butterfly

Lappet moth caterpillar (*Anthela*), Papua New Guinea

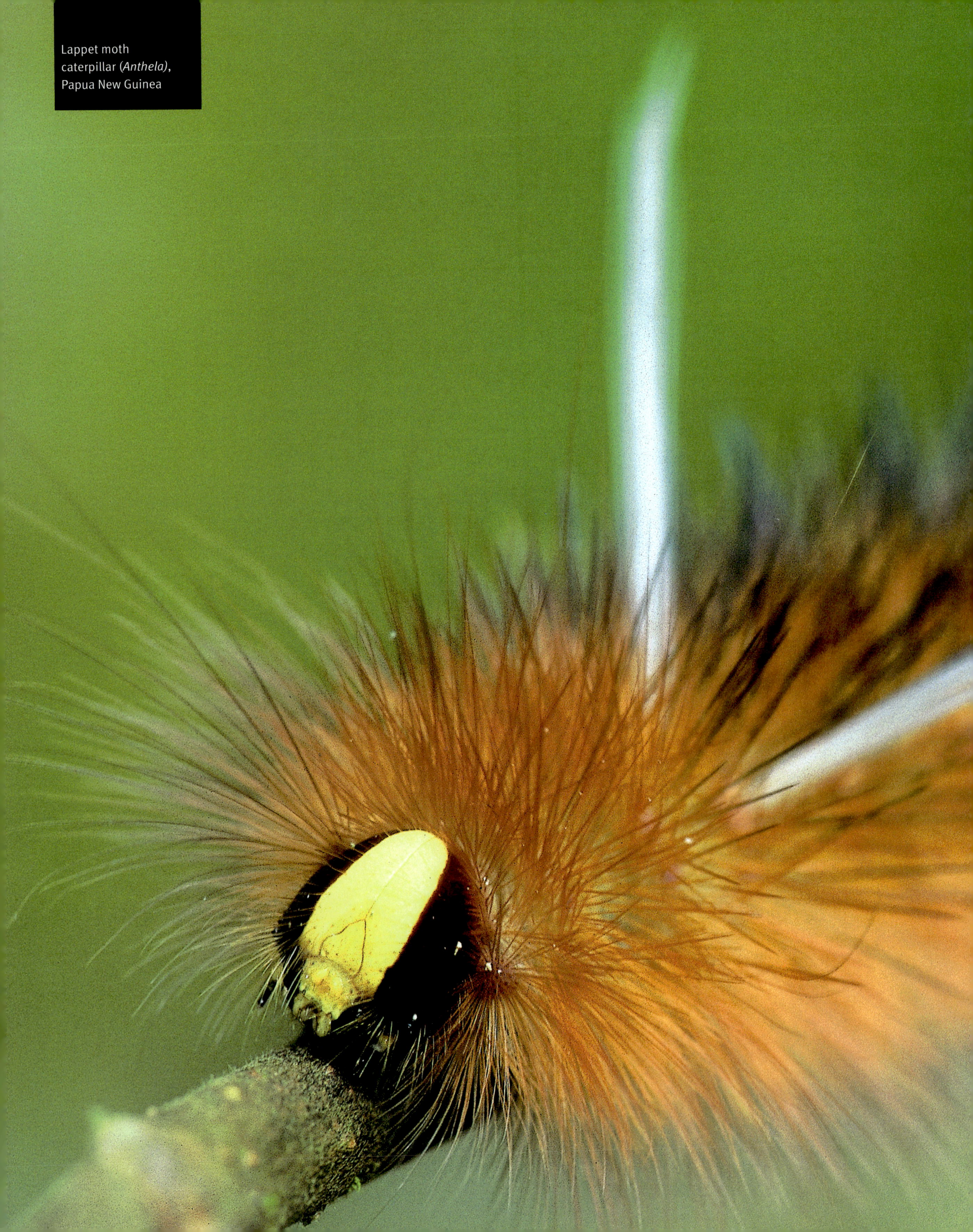

Common yellow swallow-tail caterpillar (*Papilio machaon*), Europe

Thoas swallowtail caterpillar (*Papilio thoas*), Colombia

Silver-bordered fritillary
(*Clossiana selene*),
Europe

Common rose (*Pachliopta aristolochiae*), Thailand

Red Admiral (*Vanessa atalanta*), Europe

Clearwing butterfly
(*Ithomia salapia*), Peru

Tailed green-banded
blue (*Danis cyanea*),
Australia

Banded orange
heliconians (*Dryadula
phaetusa*), Colombia

Dyson's swordtail
(*Rhetus dysonii*), Peru

Paris peacock (*Papilio paris*), Thailand

Scarce swallowtail
(*Iphiclides podalirius*),
Europe

LONDON, NEW YORK, MELBOURNE,
MUNICH, AND DELHI

PROJECT ART EDITOR Victoria Clark
DESIGN ASSISTANCE Edward Kinsey
PROJECT EDITOR Tom Broder
US EDITOR Christine Heilman

CONSULTANTS Dick Vane-Wright,
John Tennent

MANAGING EDITOR Debra Wolter
MANAGING ART EDITOR Karen Self
ART DIRECTOR Bryn Walls
PUBLISHER Jonathan Metcalf

DTP DESIGNER John Goldsmid
PRODUCTION CONTROLLER Louise Minihane
INDEXER Hilary Bird

First American Edition, 2008

Published in the United States by
DK Publishing
375 Hudson Street
New York, New York 10014

08 09 10 11   10 9 8 7 6 5 4 3 2

BD532 April 2008

Published in Great Britain by
Dorling Kindersley Limited

A catalog record for this book is available from the
Library of Congress

ISBN 978-0-7566-3340-0

DK books are available at special discounts when purchased
in bulk for sales promotions, premiums, fund-raising, or
educational use. For details, contact: DK Publishing Special
Markets, 375 Hudson Street, New York, New York 10014 or
SpecialSales@dk.com.

Reproduction in the UK by
Media Development Printing Ltd
Printed and bound in China by
Leo Paper Products Ltd

See our complete catalogue at
www.dk.com

contents

a photographer's passion

My fascination with butterflies started so early in life I can barely remember how or why it began. As a child I would search the countryside around my home in Switzerland for caterpillars. I took them back to my room and reared them indoors, entranced by the magical transformation of caterpillar to chrysalis and chrysalis to butterfly.

In the past, butterflies inspired people to become collectors. Armed with nets and poison jars, butterfly collectors scoured the countryside for rare species to capture and pin in glass cases. Today we have a different way to collect trophies: through photography. I began photographing butterflies when I was 16 and quickly became as passionate about nature photography as I am about nature. To begin with, neither pastime was a profession. I never studied biology, and I didn't make a living from photography until I was older. Until then, I used earnings from various jobs to fund trips to the world's tropical rainforests, where the greatest diversity of butterflies can be found.

One of the fascinating things about butterflies is the insight they give you into their environment. They are natural indicators, their diversity reflecting the true underlying biodiversity of their habitat. Nowhere is this more apparent than in rainforest, where hundreds of butterfly species may coexist in one small area. Such diversity can only be found in unspoiled primary forest, yet these biological hotspots are rapidly disappearing. Butterflies tell us where to focus our conservation efforts, and this is as true of temperate habitats, where the greatest diversity occurs in ancient meadows or woodlands that have escaped the ravages of intensive agriculture and pesticides. In recent years, butterflies have also become early warning signals. Thanks to the army of enthusiasts who diligently monitor the appearance of butterflies every year, we now know that many of Europe's species are being driven north by global warming.

So these captivating animals are far more than just "flying flowers" to conserve for their own sake. They embody the health of nature itself and tell us when we are winning or losing the battle to protect the natural systems on which all life depends. Let's hope they survive long into the future.

Thomas Marent

identity

what is a butterfly?

Butterflies and moths make up the order Lepidoptera, a large and diverse group of insects characterized by a range of unique anatomical features.

Butterflies charm our eyes with their captivating colors and the graceful dance of their fluttering wings. Yet their beauty is fragile and their lives are fleeting, a brief flowering that embodies the ephemeral nature of the seasons. This delicate beauty has made butterflies the most sought-after and studied of all insects. For centuries they have been hunted and collected, named and classified, argued about and fought over. Today, we know more about butterflies than about any other insects.

With over 165,000 described species, butterflies and moths make up around one in every six named species of insect. They can be found in every region of the world, in habitats as diverse as tropical rainforest and Arctic tundra. The order is termed Lepidoptera—from the Greek words for "scale" and "wing"—after one of their most notable characteristics: the tiny scales that decorate their wings with a lavish array of colors. Most butterflies and moths also possess broad membranous

△ A shepherd's fritillary (*Boloria pales*) rests on edelweiss (*Leontopodium alpinum*).
▷ Perched on a water avens (*Geum rivale*), a violet copper (*Lycaena helle*) sits with wings closed upright in typical butterfly style.

wings and a distinctive coiled proboscis. Such anatomical features provide the basis for the modern system of classification that divides the Lepidoptera into around 100 different families, including five recognized families of "true butterflies."

SCALY WINGS

Butterflies and moths owe much of their charm to their most characteristic attribute: the tiny, overlapping scales that deck their wings like sequins. Although each scale almost invariably presents a single, flat color, when arranged in a mosaic they dazzle the eye with kaleidoscopic patterns and hues. The colors are formed in two ways. Most come from chemical pigments such as melanin, which is responsible for the intense black and other deep shades of butterfly wings. Other pigments — yellows, reds, or more rarely blues — may also be derived from plants or from waste chemicals that build up during metamorphosis. Metallic or iridescent blues and greens are created not by pigments but by the microscopic architecture of the scales. A butterfly scale has an open lattice structure containing myriad reflective surfaces. The spacing of these surfaces causes reflected light waves to interfere, so that certain wavelengths are canceled out and others are enhanced, producing strong colors. Like the patterns on a soap bubble, these colors may shimmer and vary with the changing angle of view, a phenomenon known as iridescence — though butterfly scales also produce structural colors that stay constant from any angle.

▷ The wings of the Maackii peacock (*Papilio maackii*) of China feature iridescent blue and jade scales set among contrasting black scales, an optical trick that makes the colors appear more luminous.

△ Butterfly scales are modified hairs, each formed as an outgrowth from a single cell. The red eyespots of the apollo (*Parnassius apollo*) are a mosaic of red, white, and black scales.

◁ The lustrous blue of this Brazilian metalmark (*Lasaia arsis*) is a structural color, produced by the reflection of light by multiple layers within the wing scales.

▷ The underwing colors of the painted beauty butterfly (*Batesia hypochlora*) of Peru are produced by pigments such as melanin.

" One of the challenges of photographing butterflies is capturing the striking colors of the wings. Butterflies tend to close their wings on landing, and their bobbing style of flight makes it almost impossible to photograph them in the air. Fortunately, the undersides of the wings in some species are just as interesting as the upper sides. The "eighty-eights" and "eighty-nines" of tropical America have markings that look like numbers. Their fondness for dung and detritus makes them all the more easy to photograph—you can often find these dainty creatures perched on the ground sucking something repulsive. "

Callicore eunomia of Bolivia sports a number 80 on a yellow background. The upper sides of the wings provide contrast with splashes of iridescent blue and dazzling red against deep black.

△ Prola beauty (*Panacea prola*), Ecuador

△ Prola beauty (*Panacea prola*), underside of wings

△ Nymphalid butterfly (*Nessaea obrinus*), Peru

△ Nymphalid butterfly (*Nessaea obrinus*), upper sides of wings

△ Iole's daggerwing (*Marpesia iole*), Colombia

△ Iole's daggerwing (*Marpesia iole*), underside of wings

Colored scales decorate both the upper sides and the undersides of butterfly wings, but the patterns can be remarkably different. Very often the undersides are drab for camouflage, while the upper sides of the wings bear vibrant hues that signal identity to prospective mates or advertise toxicity to predators.

◁▽ This Colombian nymphalid (*Panacea procilla*) can transform itself by opening its wings to reveal a shimmering blue design. It may appear even more intense to butterfly eyes, which are sensitive to a wider spectrum of light than our own.

In common with all insects, butterflies and moths have bodies divided into three main regions: head, thorax, and abdomen. The middle section—the thorax—is the point of connection for legs and wings, and it houses powerful muscles that cause the wings to beat. The two pairs of wings are made of chitin, the same tough carbohydrate that forms an insect's body wall, but they are diaphanously thin and require a network of reinforcing veins for support. These veins are only briefly used for circulation when a butterfly emerges from the chrysalis and fluid must be pumped into the wings to make them expand. This done, the wings harden and the veins generally empty to become hollow, air-filled struts. Features of the wings that seem trivial at first glance can provide insights into the evolutionary history of butterflies and moths, and hence the way that we classify them. In butterflies, the forewings and hind wings merely overlap, with strong veins in the overlapping region to ensure that the wings beat as one. In many moths, however, a kind of catch ties the wings together. The branching pattern of the wing veins is also important: each butterfly family has a distinctive pattern that varies, on a finer scale, from species to species.

◁ Stripes of pigment emphasize the veins on the wings of this bee butterfly (*Chorinea sylphina*) in Peru.

△ In this Peruvian clearwing (*Cithaerias*) the absence of scales reveals the transparent wing membranes that all butterflies possess.

△ A dotted border (*Mylothris*) rests on moss in the Ugandan forest, revealing the delicate tracery of veins on the underside of its wings.

△ Starting life a pristine white with dark veins, the wings of *Aporia crataegi* become gradually more parchmentlike with age.

031

IDENTITY

ANTENNAE AND EYES

A butterfly's head is dominated by its main sense organs: a pair of bulbous compound eyes and a pair of antennae. The eyes are made of up to 17,000 hexagonal facets, each one a working eye in miniature. Butterfly eyes are highly sensitive to color and movement but have poor definition—they probably can't make out the detailed patterns on each other's wings. The antennae are the main organs of smell, though they can also sense air vibrations produced by nearby noise or movement. Butterflies usually have slender, clubbed antennae, while those of moths may be tapered, feathery, or serrated. Whatever their shape, antennae play a key role in courtship: male moths usually find their mates by scent, while certain male butterflies court females by sprinkling scented scale particles— "love dust"—over their partners' antennae.

◁ Butterflies such as this arctic skipper (*Carterocephalus palaemon*) wave their antennae to investigate their environment. The antennae are packed with nerve endings sensitive to airborne chemicals, allowing the butterfly to detect food and mates.

△ Positioned on either side of the head, the globelike eyes of this niobe fritillary (*Fabriciana niobe*) contain thousands of individual facets called ommatidia, providing good all-around vision.

▷ A high brown fritillary (*Fabriciana adippe*). The function of the clubbed ends of the butterfly's antennae is unclear, but they could play a role in flight control by making the antennae vibrate in response to turning forces. This information may be transmitted to the butterfly via a group of sensory cells at the base of each antenna known as Johnston's organ, to help the insect orient itself in space.

▷ Moths tend to be active by night and so rely more heavily than butterflies on smell. To maximize contact with the air, the antennae of moths such as the tau emperor (*Aglia tau*) have a feathery structure, with dozens of branches subdivided into yet more tiny filaments.

△ The black V moth (*Arctornis l-nigrum*) is named after a black checkmark on its ghostly white wings. Unlike most other moths and butterflies, the adult of this species has no proboscis and cannot feed.

▷ To aid his nocturnal hunt for females, this male lobster moth (*Stauropus fagi*) is equipped with huge, comb-shaped (pectinate) antennae, and dense hair to keep

PROBOSCIS

The majority of butterflies and moths have a purely liquid diet, favoring sugary fluids such as nectar or juices from rotting fruit. They feed with a coiled tongue called a proboscis, which works like a drinking straw. The proboscis is not simply a hollow tube. It consists of two tubes zipped tightly together by microscopic hooks, and fluids are sucked up through the space between. The whole structure has an inherent tendency to roll into a coil when not in use and so must be forcibly extended for feeding. When extended, it usually has a distinct kink about a third of the way along, allowing the butterfly to probe vertically with the tip.

◁ A hummingbird hawk moth (*Macroglossum stellatarum*) probes a wild teasel (*Dipsacus fullonum*) for nectar. Hawk moths have very long proboscises and can reach nectar deep inside flowers.

△ A purple emperor (*Apatura iris*) extends its proboscis, perhaps to sip aphid honeydew from leaves. The purple emperor does not visit flowers for nectar, preferring honeydew or sap.

▷ The elephant hawk moth (*Deilephila elpenor*) feeds on the wing, a shimmering blur of pink as it hovers around honeysuckle flowers or petunias searching for nectar with its long proboscis.

△ An orange-tip butterfly (*Anthocharis cardamines*) at rest, its long proboscis tightly coiled.

THORAX AND ABDOMEN

The thorax and abdomen of a butterfly are both divided into a series of segments, though these are not always clearly visible. Each of the three segments making up the thorax bears a pair of jointed legs. Two of the segments also bear a pair of wings. Seen close up, many butterflies and moths are surprisingly hairy around the thorax, with an almost furlike pelt that often extends to the abdomen and head. These hairs trap a layer of insulating air next to the body and so conserve the heat generated by the flight muscles, which must be warm in order to work properly. The abdomen consists of ten segments that house the digestive system toward the front and reproductive organs toward the rear. In males, the hindmost segments contain a kind of clasping mechanism used to lock on to a female's abdomen during mating. In females, the hind quarters contain a retractile organ called an ovipositor, used for laying eggs. Butterflies and moths do not have arteries and veins—instead, blood simply circulates through body cavities, driven by a single large vessel, referred to as a "heart," that runs along the length of the body.

◁ An elephant hawk moth (*Deilephila elpenor*) dangles from its perch, showing its hairy thorax. The sturdy build and dense hair help maintain body temperature at night, when the hawk moth is most active.

△ The black-rayed jewelmark (*Sarota chrysus*) of Colombia has exceptionally hairy legs for a butterfly. The caterpillars of this unusual species feed on epiphylls—tiny plants that flourish on the surface of rain-soaked leaves in the rainforest.

CLASSIFICATION

To most people, the distinction between moths and butterflies seems obvious: butterflies are day-flying insects with enchantingly colorful wings that fold upright when they land; moths are drab, nocturnal creatures whose pale wings lie flat or tentlike when they land. While this is a useful rule of thumb, it does not always stand up to scrutiny: there are day-flying moths, nocturnal butterflies, moths that are beautifully colored, butterflies that are drab and plain. A more fundamental distinction is based on subtle anatomical details, including the branching pattern of the wing veins and the shape of the antennae (slender and clubbed in butterflies).

Butterflies and moths do not form equal divisions of the Lepidoptera family tree. In reality, nearly the whole tree from trunk to twigs is taken up by moths, which make up at least 90 percent of Lepidoptera species and account for more than 90 of the 100 or so families. Butterflies evolved from moths and from an evolutionary perspective are simply a subgroup of moths. The butterflies' modest branch splits into two smaller branches, one leading to "skippers" (a family of stout-bodied butterflies that fly rather like moths) and the other to the five recognized families of "true butterflies": the Papilionidae, the Lycaenidae, the Pieridae, the Riodinidae, and the Nymphalidae.

▷ The typhla satyr (*Oressinoma typhla*) of Venezuela is a member of the true butterfly family Nymphalidae. Like other nymphalids, it appears to have only four legs, the front pair of legs being much reduced in size and not used for walking.

△ Members of the butterfly family Pieridae cluster on a patch of wet ground in Brazil in search of salts. White and yellow are dominant colors in this family.

PAPILIONIDAE

Members of this family, which includes around 600 species, are known as swallowtails because many (though not all) have tail streamers on their hind wings. Swallowtails are renowned for their beauty and size and include the world's largest butterfly, the rare Queen Alexandra's birdwing (*Ornithoptera alexandrae*) of Papua New Guinea, which has a wingspan of 10 in (25 cm). Swallowtail caterpillars have a peculiar forked organ behind the head that pops out when they feel threatened. Called an osmeterium, it is unique to the family and is thought to repel predators by releasing a pungent chemical similar to turpentine.

△ Paris peacock
(*Papilio paris*), Thailand

△ Kite swallowtail
(*Eurytides*), Venezuela

△ Tailed jay
(*Graphium agamemnon*), Indonesia

Glitterlike blue scales decorate the wings of the common yellow swallowtail (*Papilio machaon*), a species found throughout most of the northern hemisphere.

LYCAENIDAE

The Lycaenidae are a family of around 6,000 small but often brightly colored butterflies, including the blues, coppers, and hairstreaks. The family includes one of the world's smallest butterflies, the western pygmy blue (*Brephidium exilis*), which is about the size of a human thumbnail. As larvae, many lycaenids have a close relationship with ants, which they feed with sugary secretions (honeydew) and often amino acids in exchange for protection. Some caterpillars, however, have become predatory and spend part of their lives inside ant nests, either devouring their hosts' helpless grubs, or being fed directly by the ants.

▷ The purple-shot copper (*Lycaena alciphron*) is one of about 100 species of copper butterflies in the family Lycaenidae. Male coppers are often found perched in sunny spots waiting for passing females and showing off the brilliant, orange-red wings after which they are named.

△ Scarce copper (*Lycaena virgaureae*), Europe

◁ Blues are typically small grassland butterflies with iridescent blue upper wing surfaces. Not all are blue— some are brown, especially females. There are some 2,000 species that together make up a large subfamily (Polyommatinae) within the family Lycaenidae. This is a female common blue (*Polyommatus icarus*).

PIERIDAE

The family Pieridae includes the whites, yellows, sulphurs, and orange tips. As the names suggest, most of these butterflies are white or yellow. The colors often look solid to our eyes, but many pierids are thought to have ultraviolet-reflecting patterns that we cannot see. There are only 1,000 or so species in this family, yet they are among the most abundant and familiar butterflies. The caterpillars of species such as the cabbage whites are especially well known to gardeners: they are pests that feed voraciously on plants of the cabbage family (Brassicaceae).

◁ In the tropics, male pierid butterflies are often to be seen clustered on damp ground sucking salt, a habit known as puddling.

△ Small cabbage white
(*Pieris rapae*), Europe

△ Palaeno sulphur
(*Colias palaeno*), Europe

△ Painted jezebel
(*Delias hyparete*), Thailand

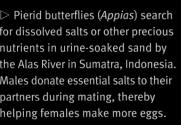
▷ Pierid butterflies (*Appias*) search for dissolved salts or other precious nutrients in urine-soaked sand by the Alas River in Sumatra, Indonesia. Males donate essential salts to their partners during mating, thereby helping females make more eggs.

RIODINIDAE

Members of this family are also known as metal-marks or jewelmarks because their wings often bear spots of gleaming metallic color. Some authorities class the Riodinidae as a subfamily of Lycaenidae, but molecular and anatomical evidence suggests they are a separate though closely related group. Like lycaenids, riodinids are mostly small and many of their larvae have a close association with ants. Most of the 1,200 or more species are found in tropical America, where they exhibit a striking range of shapes and colors, from drab mothlike creatures to some of the most beautiful of all butterflies.

▷ Like many other members of the family Riodinidae, the red harlequin (*Paralaxita telesia*) of Sumatra has exquisitely ornate wings decorated with shiny metallic marks.

△ Sword-tailed beautymark (*Rhetus arcius*), Peru

△ Metalmark (*Eurybia patrona*), Costa Rica

△ Metalmark (*Hyphilaria parthenis*), Bolivia

△ Metalmark (*Menander menander*), Bolivia

▷ The lampeto metalmark (*Caria mantinea*) of Colombia displays the sparkling metallic colors after which the metalmarks are named. Unlike many other butterflies, metalmarks often perch on leaves with their wings open and flat.

△ A map butterfly (*Araschnia levana*) uses its four functional legs to rest on a columbine seedpod (*Aquilegia vulgaris*). The disruptive pattern on the wings helps disguise the butterfly's outline when seen from a distance.

Nymphalidae contain around 6,500 species and include several large subfamilies once classed as families in their own right. These include milkweeds (Danainae), which acquire protective chemicals from plants, and satyrs (Satyrinae), which mostly feed on grasses as larvae and have and the remarkably widespread painted lady (*Vanessa cardui*), which has been found on every continent except Antarctica. Perhaps most magnificent of all is the blue morpho (*Morpho menelaus*) of South America, renowned for the dazzling brilliance of its electric-blue wings.

△ A spotted fritillary (*Melitaea didyma*) clings to a flowerhead of agrimony (*Agrimonia eupatoria*). As in many nymphalids, the bright upper sides of the butterfly's wings are offset by well-camouflaged undersides.

Tucked in below the eye of this malachite butterfly (*Siproeta steneles*) is one of its miniaturized front legs. In male nymphalids, the front legs have evolved into tiny brushlike structures, while in females they are slightly longer and are used for tasting plants.

MOTHS

From a scientific perspective, moths do not form a natural category of insects with their own family tree. They are simply the remains of the Lepidoptera family tree after the butterfly branch is cut off—there is no modern scientific term for moths. Nevertheless, moths are far more numerous, diverse, and ancient than butterflies. They vary in size from tiny "microlepidoptera" with wingspans as small as ¹/₁₀ in (3 mm), to giants such as the white witch moth (*Thysania agrippina*), whose wingspan of 11 in (28 cm) makes it the largest of all Lepidoptera. Not all moths are pale and drab. Many of the larger species—the "macrolepidoptera"—rival butterflies in their size and beauty, and some look so similar to butterflies that only expert eyes can tell them apart. Moths account for about 150,000 of the 165,000 or so known species of Lepidoptera, but the true number of moth species is probably vastly greater, since there are thought to be countless more awaiting discovery. Relative to butterflies, moths are uncharted territory for scientists. Their classification is a work in progress, with around 100 currently recognized families. Among the best known are the hawk moths (Sphingidae), a family of powerful, aerobatic fliers that beat their wings fast enough to hover like hummingbirds, and the giant silk moth family (Saturniidae), which includes some of the largest and most spectacular moths. Some owlet moths (Noctuidae) are as big as silk moths or even larger, and many have superbly camouflaged forewings that cover startlingly colorful hind wings. The tiger moth family (Arctiidae) includes many species that are active by day, when the danger of being seen by predators is greatest. Many protect themselves with noxious chemicals and advertise their qualities with colors that are as bright as any butterfly's.

▷ Ermine moths such as the buff ermine (*Spilosoma lutea*) are so named because their thick manes and black-spotted wings are reminiscent of ermine fur coats.

△ Arctiid moth (*Ischnognatha semiopalina*), French Guiana

" When you spend the night in a rainforest, you meet a lot of weird and wonderful creatures. One of the most spectacular insects you are likely to come across is a giant silk moth. They are bigger than bats and flap around lights on wings so huge you can almost hear them beat. In French Guiana I stayed in a small hostel where we had to sleep in hammocks. A scientist at the hostel had set up a special light and a white sheet to capture moths in the night. Early the next morning I had a look around the capture site and discovered this striking beauty resting on a leaf with just enough soft morning light to take a photograph. "

◁ The wings of this male giant silk moth (*Rothschildia hesperus*) of South America are almost as large as a pair of human hands, but it is not the largest member of the family Saturniidae. The atlas moth (*Attacus atlas*) of Southeast Asia has a wingspan of 10 in (25 cm) and possibly the largest total wing area of any insect.

△ Geometer moth (*Rhodochlora rufaria*), French Guiana

△ Butterfly moth (*Callidula*), Malaysia

△ Swallowtail moth (*Urania leilus*), Bolivia

△ Tiger moth (*Pachydota nervosa*), Peru

△ Geometer moth (*Pantherodes*), Peru

△ Hawk moth (*Protambulyx goeldii*), French Guiana

before a female butterfly dies, her most important task is to find a home for her offspring. An orange tip (*Anthocharis cardamines*) does this with utmost care, flying slowly and deliberately through meadows and forest glades as she searches for particular plants. She is drawn to the dainty flowers of plants belonging to the wild mustard family. When she sees one, she checks it for butterfly eggs. If there are none, she alights near the flowers and tastes the plant with sensory hairs on her feet. All being well, she glues a single egg to the flowerhead and departs. Nourished by a protein-rich yolk

and fat reserves, a caterpillar grows inside the tough, waterproof eggshell. Butterfly eggs can stay dormant for months in cold weather, but in the warmth of summer a caterpillar may be ready to emerge in under a week, its tightly coiled body filling the egg. It frees itself by biting its way out. Some butterflies lay their eggs in batches, and when the caterpillars emerge they cluster together for safety. Not so the orange tip. It lays a single egg on each plant because the caterpillars feed only on the flowerheads, which are in short supply. If the caterpillar finds a young rival on its plant, it will cannibalize it.

◁▽ Orange tip butterflies (*Anthocharis cardamines*) lay their eggs singly, fixing each one with a smear of glue to the flowerhead of a cuckooflower (*Cardamine pratensis*) or garlic mustard (*Alliaria petiolata*).

△ As an orange tip caterpillar develops, its body color shows through the transparent shell and the egg darkens.

△ An orange tip's first meal is its eggshell. Not all caterpillars eat their eggshell, but some will die if deprived of it.

△ Puss moth (*Cerura vinula*), Europe

△ Painted lady (*Vanessa cardui*), Europe

△ Broad-bordered bee hawkmoth
(*Hemaris fuciformis*), Europe

△ Almond-eyed ringlet (*Erebia alberganus*), Europe

△ Apollo (*Parnassius apollo*), Europe

△ Emperor moth (*Saturnia pavonia*), Europe

△ False ringlet (*Coenonympha oedippus*), Europe

△ Fox moth (*Macrothylacia rubi*), Europe

Butterfly and moth eggs vary enormously in color, texture, and shape. Some are smooth as pearls; others bear exquisite, sculpted patterns imprinted by the mother's ovarioles. At the top of each egg there is usually a slight indentation and a tiny hole— the micropyle— where the sperm entered to fertilize the egg before it was laid.

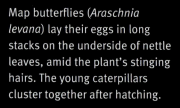

Map butterflies (*Araschnia levana*) lay their eggs in long stacks on the underside of nettle leaves, amid the plant's stinging hairs. The young caterpillars cluster together after hatching.

Kentish glory moths (*Endromis versicolora*) lay their eggs on birch twigs, the eggs hatching in spring as the tree's buds burst open. The caterpillars are black at first, but become a vivid green color after molting. Clustered together on twigs, they resemble birch catkins.

EATING MACHINES

In order to stand a chance of becoming a healthy adult, a caterpillar must multiply in weight about a thousandfold in as little as two weeks. So from the moment it hatches, a caterpillar needs to eat almost nonstop. Equipped for a life of consumption, its body is radically different from that of the adult in almost every respect. In place of the coiled feeding tube are two pairs of serrated jaws that slice together sideways like shears to macerate plant matter. Powerful jaw muscles fill the head, and digestive organs take up much of the body's volume. The adult's large compound eyes are missing; instead there are two rows of tiny, simple eyes on the sides of the head that see little more than light and shade. These are flanked by stumpy, downward-pointing antennae that help the nearly blind caterpillar sense its way around the plant.

◁ Bristling with defensive spines, the caterpillar of a Peruvian saturniid moth (*Gamelia*) consumes a leaf edge-first. Large caterpillars typically feed on the outside of plants, but the larvae of many small moths burrow within the leaves or plant stems.

△ Tiny black eyes, red jaws, and pink-tipped antennae are clearly visible on the head of this poplar hawkmoth caterpillar (*Laothoe populi*).

FOOTWORK

All insects have six legs, yet at first glance caterpillars appear to have many more. Close inspection reveals that the first six are small and clawlike, while the rest are fat and fleshy and seem to end in suckers. The front six are true jointed legs and foreshadow the legs of the adult insect. Caterpillars often use them more like hands than feet, gripping on to leaves while their jaws cut the leaves to shreds. The fleshy rear legs, called false legs or prolegs, are used for walking and climbing. They disappear completely in the pupa, the tissue digested and recycled elsewhere in the body. At the base of each proleg is a flat foot covered in tiny hooks that grip nooks and crannies in leaves. A muscle within each proleg can pull the center of the foot inward, digging in the hooks and tightening the foot's grip. Most caterpillars have ten prolegs, the last two serving as claspers. However, some get by with fewer: geometrid moth caterpillars have only one or two pairs and move by looping their body rather than shuffling their feet.

△ A Peruvian saturniid moth caterpillar (*Automeris*) grips a twig with true legs (red) and false legs (black and red). The minute hooks covering the base of the false legs are just visible.

◁ Like most caterpillars, swallowtails (*Papilio machaon*) use their front legs to grip on to food as they feed.

In contrast to the small true legs, caterpillars' false legs (prolegs) are jointless, fleshy extensions of body segments. This Peruvian *Automeris* moth caterpillar also possesses a formidable arsenal of irritating spines.

◁ Despite having only one or two pairs of prolegs, geometrid moths (Geometridae) are among the most acrobatic of caterpillars. Both front and rear legs clasp with sufficient strength to support the whole body weight, enabling the caterpillar to walk by looping or stretch out rigid to resemble a broken twig.

△ Gripping tightly onto a twig with its fleshy prolegs, a coxcomb prominent (*Ptilodon capucina*) bends backward in its defensive posture.

△ Though brightly colored, the caterpillar of Australia's four o'clock moth (*Dysphania fenestrata*) looks like a yellow catkin when it dangles from its claspers.

△▷ Also known as inchworms, loopers, and measuring worms, geometrid moth caterpillars such as this mottled umber (*Erannis defoliaria*) appear to be measuring their progress as they move along, seemingly inch by inch, with loops of the body. The family name Geometridae has the same Greek root as "geometry" and means "land measurers."

△ The loose folds of translucent green skin of this kentish glory
(*Endromis versicolora*) will fill out as the caterpillar grows.

SKIN

All insects are endowed with a tough external skeleton, or exoskeleton, and caterpillars are no exception. Although the skin of a caterpillar is much less rigid than the exoskeleton of most insects, it is not as elastic as it appears and it cannot grow. Loose folds allow some room for expansion, but eventually a limit is reached and the caterpillar must shed its skin. The only rigid parts of the exoskeleton are around the head, the true legs, and the spiracles (breathing pores) that run along both sides of the body.

△ Pink spiracles, diagonal yellow stripes, and a mass of tiny yellow nodules adorn the jade skin of the poplar hawk moth (*Laothoe populi*).

The white spots on the skin of the kentish glory (*Endromis versicolora*) are spiracles, or breathing holes. Insects do not have lungs. Instead, their bodies are riddled with a network of air tubes linked to the outside world by the spiracles.

△▷ The skin of large moth caterpillars is often decorated with colorful warts and irritating spines. The curious warts on the giant peacock (*Saturnia pyri*)—the largest of Europe's butterflies and moths—change color with each molt. First brown, they then turn yellow, pink, and finally sky blue.

Some caterpillars' bodies are embellished by elaborate flaps, horns, and other puzzling protuberances. The hawk moth caterpillar (Sphingidae) has a tapering horn at the rear, varying from a small button to a spindly thread as long as the body. Its function is a mystery. It could be the relic of a more complete set of defensive spines that covered the body of some distant ancestor, but if so, why hasn't evolution gotten rid of it? Perhaps predators mistake it for a stinger or confuse it with a leaf stalk. Other adornments serve a more obvious defensive purpose. Swallowtail caterpillars (Papilionidae) possess a forked gland known as an osmeterium behind the head. Normally concealed within a pouch, it turns inside-out like a sock when the caterpillar is alarmed and releases a repulsive odor. Certain lycaenid caterpillars that live in partnership with ants possess brushlike organs that pop up when the caterpillar is distressed and release an alarm scent, rallying support from pugnacious soldier ants.

▷ As well as the taillike horn, the death's-head hawkmoth (*Acherontia atropos*) has several other peculiar features. The adults can squeak like mice and their dark bodies appear to bear the ghostly image of a human skull.

▷ Hawkmoth caterpillars such as the spurge hawkmoth (*Hyles euphorbiae*) are sometimes known as hornworms because of the mysterious horn at their rear end.

△ A scarce swallowtail (*Iphiclides podalirius*) deploys its osmeterium. Glistening with foul-smelling fluid, this defensive gland probably serves to repel predatory insects such as wasps.

△ Slug caterpillar
(Limacodidae), Thailand

△ Owlet moth caterpillar
Hemiceras), Peru

△ Arctiid moth caterpillar
(Arctiidae), Peru

△ Privet hawkmoth
(*Sphinx ligustri*), Europe

△ Slug caterpillar (Limacodidae),
Papua New Guinea

" In the Peruvian rainforest, a biologist told me about some beautiful morpho caterpillars she'd seen on a tree. It was off the trail, but she gave me directions and I found them. When I tried to return, I couldn't find the trail. Half an hour later I was back at the tree—I was walking in circles. Getting lost in the rainforest can be deadly. I began to panic and screamed for help, but there was no answer. I tried to calm down. I decided to walk along straight lines radiating from the tree, marking branches every 10 steps with a penknife so I could retrace my steps. On the third line, I found my way back to the trail. "

△ Coxcomb prominent (*Ptilodon capucina*), Europe

△ The drinker (*Euthrix potatoria*), Europe

A thick pelt of hair has earned the caterpillars of tussock moths and tiger moths the nickname "woolly bears." These hairs might help to protect the caterpillars from parasitic wasps that inject their eggs into other insects' bodies. Once hatched, the wasp larvae consume their living hosts from the inside.

◁ Monkey moth caterpillar (Eupterotidae), Thailand

△ Silk moth caterpillar (*Apatelodes firmiana*), Bolivia

△ Pale tussock (*Calliteara pudibunda*), Europe

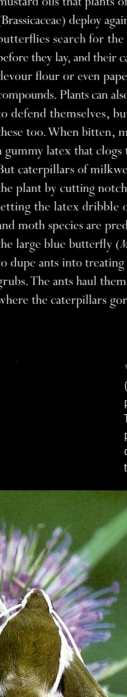

DISCERNING DIETS

Caterpillars may be gluttons, but they can be very particular about what they eat. The tobacco hornworm caterpillar (*Manduca sexta*) can digest many types of plant, but once it has tasted tobacco it will touch nothing else and would rather starve than change its diet. Such refined tastes, common among butterflies and moths, are a consequence of an evolutionary war waged by plants against their enemies. Plants do not benefit from being eaten, so they lace their tissues with poisonous or indigestible chemicals. But insects may evolve immunity and so crack a particular plant's defenses. In doing so, such insects become specialist feeders, and the poison becomes an attractant rather than a deterrent. Cabbage white butterflies (*Pieris rapae*) have evolved immunity to the hot and peppery mustard oils that plants of the cabbage family (Brassicaceae) deploy against herbivores. Female butterflies search for the taste of mustard oil before they lay, and their caterpillars will greedily devour flour or even paper smeared with these compounds. Plants can also use physical weapons to defend themselves, but insects can crack these too. When bitten, milkweed leaves exude a gummy latex that clogs the mouths of insects. But caterpillars of milkweed butterflies disarm the plant by cutting notches in leafstalks and letting the latex dribble out. A few butterfly and moth species are predatory. Caterpillars of the large blue butterfly (*Maculinea arion*) appear to dupe ants into treating them like giant ant grubs. The ants haul them back into their nest, where the caterpillars gorge on real ant larvae.

▽▷ Spurge hawkmoth caterpillars (*Hyles euphorbiae*) feed only on poisonous spurge plants (*Euphorbia*). The caterpillars use the plant's poison for their own defense and can vomit a slurry of half-digested, toxic leaves when distressed.

Columbine moth larvae (*Lamprotes c-aureum*) feed only on meadow rue (*Thalictrum*) and columbine (*Aquilegia*), plants found on damp, shady riversides and wetlands.

114

TRANSFORMATION

▷ Oak processionary moths
(*Thaumetopoea processionea*) are
named after their caterpillars, which
are sometimes seen marching in
single file along the ground. The
gregarious caterpillars are protected
by irritating hairs that interlace when
they cluster together, forming an
impregnable barrier to predators.

△▷ Caterpillars of the bird cherry ermine moth gradually extend their silk web as the colony's territory expands, in some cases covering an entire tree. The sight of hundreds of silk cocoons hanging inside the web later in the season is equally spectacular. For unknown reasons, the moth's numbers fluctuate, and in some years the webs are barely noticeable.

Caterpillars of the bird cherry ermine moth (*Yponomeuta evonymella*) dangle from their communal silk web. The web provides protection from birds while the caterpillars feed on the leaves within.

caterpillar can more than double its weight every two days. A human baby growing at such a prodigious rate would reach a ton in two weeks. Loose folds of skin allow some room for expansion, but when this slack is used up, the caterpillar must molt. First, a new exoskeleton forms under the existing one. The developing exoskeleton secretes enzymes that digest the old skin from within,

recycling precious nutrients. As much as 90 percent of the old skin is reabsorbed this way, until all that remains is a dry husk. The caterpillar is now ready to molt. It stops feeding and flexes its muscles, splitting the old skin, and then wriggles out headfirst. Before the new skin dries and hardens, the caterpillar takes in air to help inflate its body, stretching the soft skin to create room for further growth. Most caterpillars molt four

times, and the five stages between molts are known as "instars." For many species, molting is more than just a prerequisite for growth—it is a time of transformation. Body color may change dramatically from one instar to the next. Lurid spots or stripes may appear on a previously inconspicuous body; hairs, warts, or horns may sprout or vanish. Even diet and behavior can change, with some caterpillars abandoning plant food and turning carnivorous.

◁▽ Starting life a drab black, the spurge hawkmoth (*Hyles euphorbiae*) becomes green and brightly patterned after the first molt. Each successive molt brings more lurid colors, the feet and horns turning orange before the whole body finally turns blood red.

In its final incarnation, the spurge hawkmoth caterpillar (*Hyles euphorbiae*) becomes a startling red and black. The vivid colors are a warning: the caterpillar's body is packed with poisonous spurge leaves.

> I was searching for butterflies on the edge of a Swiss forest when I saw a bird-dropping on an alder leaf. It was only when I got very close that I realized with a shock that it was a living caterpillar, a perfect mimic. Exactly like the real thing, it was curled into a backward-facing question mark, one-third of its body white and two-thirds black. Intrigued, I took it home and supplied it with alder leaves while I tried to find out what it was. I couldn't believe my eyes when the repulsive-looking thing split its skin and transformed itself into an object of beauty. Since then, the alder moth has been my favorite European caterpillar, despite the adult's being a rather drab gray moth.

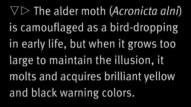

▽▷ The alder moth (*Acronicta alni*) is camouflaged as a bird-dropping in early life, but when it grows too large to maintain the illusion, it molts and acquires brilliant yellow and black warning colors.

△ Black at first, the emperor moth caterpillar (*Saturnia pavonia*) becomes more brightly patterned with each molt.

△ By the time the caterpillar has molted three times, he skin becomes a blotchy mix of green and black.

△ After the fourth molt, the caterpillar's skin is mostly green and warts are outlined in black.

▷ The full-grown emperor moth caterpillar is green with black hoops over yellow warts. At close range, the bold colors make its defensive warts more alarming. From a distance, the same pattern provides effective camouflage

" I was photographing alpine plants in the Swiss mountains when I came across something I'd wanted to see since I was a boy: a lobster moth caterpillar, surely one of the strangest caterpillars that exists. It was sitting in its classic defensive pose, with head arched back and abdomen folded to display the two differently colored tails – one of the animal world's rare examples of asymmetry. But there was something odd. The caterpillar wasn't on its usual food plant (beech) and it kept remarkably still while I photographed it. When I returned a few days later I discovered what was wrong. The caterpillar was dead and its body was riddled with hundreds of tiny parasites. "

▽▷ Newly hatched lobster moth caterpillars (*Stauropus fagi*) appear to mimic ants. After their first and second molts they resemble scorpions or mantises; as they reach maturity they look more like lobsters. When threatened, they rear up in a menacing pose and brandish their extraordinarily long front legs.

Feeding time is over for this plump swallowtail caterpillar (*Papilio machaon*). Having gorged itself for several weeks on its food plant it is now ready to tie itself to the stem with a silk harness and shed its skin for the very last time.

With its rear claspers anchored
to a silk tether and a girdle of silk
encircling its body, the swallowtail
caterpillar (*Papilio machaon*) splits
open to reveal the chrysalis within.
Able only to wriggle, the chrysalis
works the skin down to its tail end.
The tail end then lifts briefly to cast
off the skin and reattaches, held
fast by a set of tiny hooks.

A six-spot burnet moth (*Zygaena filipendulae*) starts work on the silk cocoon that will protect the pupa during metamorphosis. The largest cocoons contain up to two-thirds of a mile (1 km) of silk in a single unbroken thread.

△ Black arches (*Lymantria monacha*), Europe

△ Bagworm moth (Psychidae), Europe

△ Bath white (*Pontia daplidice*), Europe

△ Marbled fritillary (*Brenthis daphne*), Europe

△ White admiral (*Limenitis camilla*), Europe

△ Swallowtail (*Papilio machaon*), Europe

△ Marbled white (*Melanargia galathea*), Europe

△ Convolvulus hawkmoth (*Agrius convolvuli*), Europe   △ Bagworm moth (Psychidae), Europe

△ Brimstone male (*Gonepteryx rhamni*), Europe

△ Spotted fritillary (*Melitaea didyma*), Europe

Butterfly and moth pupae are surprisingly diverse in color and shape, but most are camouflaged. Immobility aids their defense, since birds and other predators spot prey by movement. Some pupae can also wriggle alarmingly when handled.

The gleaming, mirrorlike sides of the orange-spotted tiger clearwing pupa (*Mechanitis polymnia*) in Colombia provide camouflage by reflecting the light and colors of the surrounding rainforest. After a rainfall they seem to disappear among the glistening wet leaves.

142

Many chrysalises vary in color with the season or take on the hues of their surroundings for camouflage: green for fresh spring foliage; brown or gray for bark. As the chrysalis of the orange tip butterfly (*Anthocharis cardamines*) nears maturity, the bright orange pigment of the wings shows through the case.

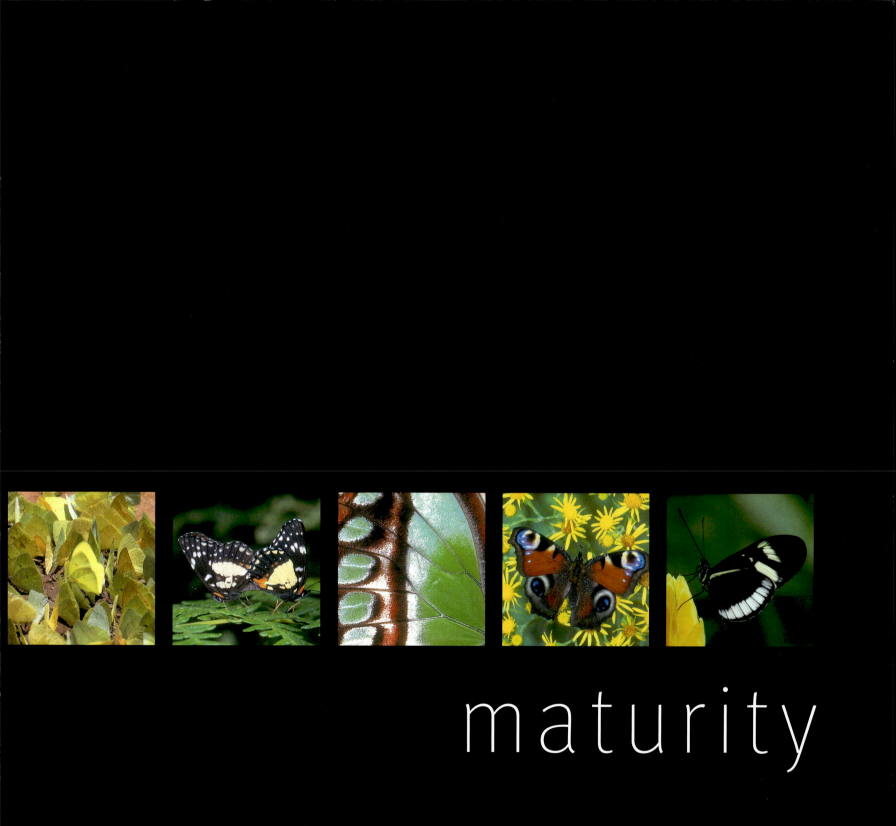

maturity

lives and behavior

From the moment they emerge from the chrysalis, the short adult lives of butterflies and moths are dedicated almost entirely to reproduction.

The brief, final flowering of the life cycle begins with the butterfly's emergence from the chrysalis. As the dry case splits, the enchanting colors of the creature within become clear. With a valiant struggle the tiny insect pulls itself free and then waits, frail and vulnerable, for its crumpled wings to unfurl like petals. The fragility of butterflies is part of their charm. Delicate and slow in flight, they seem endearingly tame as they bob from flower to flower, their lives seemingly devoted to beauty.

The impression is misleading—the lives of butterflies can be every bit as brutal and capricious as those of other animals. Their main objective in life is to pass on their genes to a new generation, and to do so, male butterflies may woo their partners with love potions derived from poisonous chemicals or entice them with precious minerals gathered from less than savory sources. Some butterflies dispense with seduction altogether, instead taking their partners by force. Reproduction need not

△ This iridescent South American nymphalid butterfly (*Asterope leprieuri*) uses its long proboscis to collect minerals concentrated by evaporation. ▷ A recently emerged swallowtail (*Papilio machaon*) pauses for a moment atop its empty chrysalis as it prepares to take flight.

take long, so a butterfly's life is usually brief. Many live only as long as it takes to mate and lay eggs, and then die; even the longest-living butterflies lead active lives that last for only a few short months.

A NEW BEGINNING

The pupal stage of a butterfly's life may be as brief as a week or as long as a year. In temperate parts of the world, where many butterfly pupae endure winter in a state of suspended animation (diapause), the warmth and lengthening days of spring are cues to awaken. Confined inside the brittle pupal case, the butterfly increases blood pressure and takes in air to inflate its body, splitting the case along lines of weakness around the head. Struggling out headfirst, the butterfly may rest halfway. Damp and shriveled, it must now perch where there is sufficient room for its wings to expand, otherwise they will harden while folded and cripple the butterfly. As it waits for its wings to open and its skin to harden, the butterfly voids waste materials that built up within the pupa, squirting out a jet of orange or blood-red fluid—meconium—from its anus. An hour or so after emerging, it is ready to fly, and with a flap of its wings it is gone.

▷ Perched on a wild carrot plant (*Daucus carota*), the adult swallowtail opens pristine wings and basks in the sun to warm its body in preparation for flight.

△ Body fluids are pumped into the wing veins to make the wings expand.

△ The newly emerged swallowtail (*Papilio machaon*) perches above its pupal case.

△ As the wings expand, air is pumped

TAKING FLIGHT

Flight brings the butterfly many advantages, liberating it from the confines of the caterpillar's world and creating new opportunities to find food and mates or evade predators. But there are conditions attached to this mode of travel. Flight consumes energy quickly, so a butterfly must refuel regularly if it is to survive more than a few days. The flight muscles must be warmed to around 85°F (30°C) to function effectively, which places temperate species in particular at the mercy of the weather. Consequently, many are sun-worshippers, often seen basking in the sun or flitting from one sunny spot to the next. The style of flight varies from one species to another. Many nymphalid butterflies have an elegant, floating manner of flight with frequent swoops and glides. In contrast, whites and many other pierid butterflies have an erratic, tumbling flight style that makes them zigzag unpredictably, confounding birds that hunt on the wing.

◁ Sharing its perch with a hoverfly, a dew-covered common blue (*Polyommatus icarus*) waits for the morning sun to dry its wings and warm its body for flight.

△ A damon blue (*Polyommatus damon*) basks on meadow clary (*Salvia pratensis*), its wings angled to catch the light.

△ Wings fully open, a marsh fritillary (*Euphydryas aurinia*) exposes the heat-absorbing pigment of its dark body to the sun's rays.

◁ A male common mormon (*Papilio polytes*) flutters under a female in an aerial courtship dance. Swooping and hovering maneuvers often play a central role in butterfly courtship, allowing partners to inspect one another and exchange scent. Female common mormons exist in three different varieties, one like the male, the other two more brightly colored.

▽ A narrow green-bordered swallowtail (*Papilio nireus*) alights on milkweed (*Asclepias*). A strong flier, this butterfly is often seen in the forests of southern and central Africa zigzagging rapidly over the ground, settling only to feed.

△ Red helen (*Papilio helenus*), India

A cloud of whites (*Appias*) erupts from the bank of the Alas River in Indonesia. Unlike smaller insects, which move their wings horizontally in a figure-eight, butterflies beat their broad wings up and down.

FEEDING

The dietary requirements of caterpillars and butterflies are very different. Caterpillars consume prodigious quantities of low-grade plant food and have a bulky, complex digestive system in order to extract the nutrients required for growth and development. Adult butterflies, in contrast, cannot grow and must in any case remain lightweight for flight, so the digestive system is simplified. They feed mostly on high-energy, liquid foods that replenish energy and water reserves. Flower nectar is ideal. At about 25 percent sugar, it provides the energy needed to power flight in a simple chemical form that demands little from the digestive system. Not all butterflies feed on flowers, though. Many prefer the sugary fluids that ooze from rotten or damaged fruit, fresh fruit being impenetrable to the delicate proboscises of most species. Others find sustenance in honeydew, the sweet, sugary excrement of sap-sucking bugs such as aphids.

◁ A cardinal (*Argynnis pandora*) searches for nectar in a thistle. A native of Mediterranean countries, the cardinal relies on nectar as a principal source of water during hot summer months.

△ A clouded yellow (*Colias croceus*) works its proboscis into red clover (*Trifolium pratense*).

▷ A mountain clouded yellow (*Colias phicomone*) feeds on heather (*Calluna vulgaris*), a plant common in the butterfly's alpine habitat.

△ Most butterflies specialize in feeding on either flowers or fallen fruit, but these red admiral butterflies (*Vanessa atalanta*) are equally happy on both.

▷ A well-camouflaged leafwing
(*Anaea nessus*) feeds on the damp
wood fibers of a fallen tree in the
Peruvian rainforest, perhaps
attracted by the tree's sweet sap.

DIETARY SUPPLEMENTS

Though rich in sugar, nectar is deficient in most other nutrients. Many butterflies make up for the shortfall by taking fluids from organic remains or from wet ground where mineral salts have been concentrated by evaporation. One highly prized mineral is sodium, which is vital for a butterfly's nervous system but is in limited supply in the foods eaten by caterpillars. Sodium is abundant in sweat and urine, both of which are sucked up avidly by many butterflies. Even bare rock can yield a valuable dose of salt if the butterfly first applies a dab of moistening saliva. Many tropical butterflies and moths are also strongly attracted to sources of decomposing protein, such as carrion or carnivore dung. The moisture in such materials contains amino acids missing from the butterfly's usual diet. Some species visit seeping wounds or runny eyes for salt or protein, and certain owlet moths can pierce skin to get at blood. The need for these unsavory supplements is greatest in males, who must provide females with a "nuptial gift" of nutrients to accompany their sperm.

▽▷ Butterflies can often be found perched on damp ground sucking up dissolved minerals using their long proboscises. Some butterflies, such as this caerulean (*Jamides*) in Borneo, are attracted to decomposing organic matter such as bird droppings.

△ Amphiro redring (*Pyrrhogyra amphiro*), Colombia

△ Eighty-eight (*Callicore*), Brazil

△ Dartwhite (*Catasticta*), Peru

△ Bee butterfly (*Chorinea amazon*), Peru

The habit of sucking up fluid from pools or damp ground is known as "puddling." Puddling butterflies can often be seen ejecting waste water from the anus while simultaneously taking in more with the proboscis. It is thought that essential minerals are extracted from the water as it passes through the butterfly's body.

△ A white dragontail (*Lamproptera curius*) expels a jet of waste water while puddling in Thailand.

△ As a white (*Hesperocharis marchalii*) sucks on damp ground in Peru, a bead of waste water forms at the tip of its abdomen.

△ Piper (*Epiphele dinora*), Peru

△ Glasswing (*Pteronymia ozia*), Peru

△ Eighty-eight (*Callicore lyca*), Colombia

△ Malayan crow (*Euploea camaralzeman*), Thailand

△ Jeweled nawab (*Polyura delphis*), Thailand

PUDDLING SITES

Butterflies find good puddling sites by watching each other. Once a fresh patch of urine or a salty puddle is discovered, it can quickly draw a crowd known colloquially as a "puddle club." In the tropics, these gatherings can sometimes contain spectacular numbers of butterflies, usually male and often neatly segregated by color or species. The mass of grounded butterflies might appear vulnerable to predators, but the insects benefit from safety in numbers. With so many eyes watching for danger, a predator is unlikely to get close without being seen. If the butterflies are disturbed, they boil up from the ground *en masse* in a dizzying cloud of wings.

▷ Groups of puddling butterflies are often dominated by whites or swallowtails. Here, a mixture of swallowtails (including *Papilio* and *Graphium*) feed by a stream in Borneo, perhaps seeking minerals concentrated by evaporation.

△ A fivebar swordtail (*Graphium antiphates*), a member of the swallowtail family, feeds on damp sand in Borneo.

can use to make butterflies easier to work with. One is to offer a bead of sweat on a finger. Once it tastes the salty fluid, a butterfly will become quite tame and can easily be placed on a flower. In rainforests, a great way to draw butterflies out of the canopy is to urinate on the ground. In Sumatra, I answered the call of nature while exploring the Alas River and returned an hour later to discover hundreds of whites sucking greedily at the damp sand. When I got close, the butterflies rose up like a cloud of snowflakes, only to tumble back down again after I backed off. 🙶

▷ Whites (*Appias*) congregate on urine-soaked sand on the bank of the Alas River in Sumatra, Indonesia.

△ A pair of common bluebottles (*Graphium sarpedon*) feed on damp gravel by a river in Thailand.

△ Groups of puddling butterflies can contain a variety of species, especially in the tropics. Here, kite swallowtails (blue and black) join a crowd dominated by whites and other pierids (mostly *Appias*).

Kite swallowtails (*Eurytides*) probe damp mud for moisture and possibly minerals in the Amazon. Beads of excreted water are visible at the tips of their abdomens.

◁ Several species of acraeine butterfly (including *Altinote negra*, *Altinote dicaeus*, and *Abanote erinome*) search a dry riverbed in Peru for salts or other substances concentrated by evaporation.

▽ Even domestic waste can provide butterflies with valuable salts. Here, acraeine butterflies feed on a boulder used by local villagers for beating laundry, perhaps drawn to minerals in the residue of laundry detergent.

❝ Some butterflies become remarkably docile while feeding on minerals, their senses dulled as though they are somehow drugged by the liquid. In Peru I saw a group of acraeine butterflies sitting on a gravel road sucking moisture from the ground. These butterflies are relatively fearless at the best of times, being well protected by cyanide chemicals and bright warning colors. This group made no attempt to escape the approaching traffic, and many were simply crushed underneath the wheels of passing trucks. ❞

Many butterflies live out their short lives within a few hundred yards of where they are born, but others embark on journeys of epic proportions, crossing entire continents and seas. Painted ladies (*Vanessa cardui*) leave their winter homes in North Africa each spring and cross the Mediterranean to Europe. Over the course of each season there may be several generations, and each one colonizes more land, eventually reaching as far north as Finland. In a similar way, the monarch butterfly (*Danaus plexippus*) repopulates eastern North America every year after spreading north from Mexico. In fall, the entire population east of the Rocky Mountains returns south in a flight of over 1,800 miles (3,000 km), completed by a single generation. Guided by instinct, stopping only to sleep or refuel with nectar, their destination is a remote area of central Mexico, where hundreds of millions of monarchs gather in a few patches of highland fir forest. Here, the butterflies are safe from frost yet cool enough to spend most of the winter semi-dormant.

▽▷ Roosting monarchs (*Danaus plexippus*) cover an oyamel fir tree (*Abies religiosa*) in Mexico. With up to 100,000 butterflies per tree, a single acre of forest can contain up to 5 million monarchs.

On warm days the roosting monarchs become active and take to the air by the thousand to find water. In spring they become sexually mature and a period of matings takes place before the butterflies leave to return north.

males, who typically use one of two techniques to find female partners: perching and patrolling. Perchers simply wait for females at a conspicuous landmark, such as a hilltop or a sunny clearing. Should a rival male appear, the resident drives the intruder away in an aerial skirmish, the two butterflies whirling around each other as they try to establish territorial rights. Patrollers hunt for females by cruising through known haunts, in food plants in case a virgin female should emerge. Once a male and female have found each other, the courtship begins. The first stage often takes place in the air, the male looping under and in front of the female so that his scent will drift across her antennae. Next, the couple may alight and engage in an elaborate sequence of bows, wing flutters, and antenna taps. If the female is suitably impressed, she may consent to mate.

▷ Male orange tips (*Anthocharis cardamines*) "patrol" for mates, flying up and down woodland edges and fencerows in search of females. Males have a flash of orange on the wings, the color perhaps serving to attract females or intimidate rivals.

△ The small tortoiseshell (*Aglais urticae*) is a "percher." The male sits guarding his territory and swoops down to drive away intruding males or court females.

△ Small tortoiseshell (*Aglais urticae*), undersides of wings

△ Thor's fritillary (*Clossiana thore*), undersides of wings

△ Thor's fritillary (*Clossiana thore*) is a "patroller." The males cruise over sunny meadows in midsummer, searching for females in the tall grass.

◁ For many butterflies, scent is at least as important in courtship as visual signals such as wing color. The dark stripes on the forewings of the male silver-washed fritillary (*Argynnis paphia*) are areas of scented scales called androconia. During courtship, the male brushes his wings across the antennae of the female to transfer his scent.

▷ Perched on a walnut tree, a male luna moth (*Actias selene*) waits for a female's scent to drift across his feathery antennae. Female luna moths "call" males in the night by extruding a scent gland at the tip of the abdomen. Males can detect the scent from a few miles away and react by flying doggedly upwind along the scent trail.

△ Male eros blue (*Polyommatus eros*), Europe

△ Female eros blue (*Polyommatus eros*), Europe

△ Male spotted fritillary (*Melitaea didyma*), Europe

△ Female spotted fritillary (*Melitaea didyma*), Europe

△ Female scarce copper (*Lycaena virgaureae*), Europe

△ Male scarce copper (*Lycaena virgaureae*), Europe

In some butterfly species, males and females are almost identical; in others the males are much more brightly colored. The evolution of gaudy males is something of a puzzle, as there is scant evidence that females prefer colorful mates. Possibly these bright male colors evolved, in some cases at least, to intimidate rival males.

△ Female chalkhill blue (*Polyommatus coridon*), Europe

" In Ticino, the Italian part of Switzerland, I was lucky enough to capture a rare sight: the courtship of the brimstone butterfly. The female adopted the classic rejection posture of pierid butterflies, her abdomen raised and her wings spread. Although it looks much like a come-on, this posture makes it impossible for the male to reach her abdomen to mate. Not all male butterflies allow the female any choice. Male monarch butterflies wrestle their partners to the ground and force them to take a lancelike penis that can cause serious injury if misdirected. Some passionvine butterflies do not even wait for their partners to emerge from the pupa: the male simply thrusts in his abdomen the moment the skin splits. "

▽▷ A female brimstone butterfly (*Gonepteryx rhamni*) spurns a male's advances, raising her abdomen over her wings to place it out of reach of his abdomen and penis.

△ Spotted fritillaries (*Melitaea didyma*), Europe

△ Mazarine blues (*Cyaniris semiargus*), Europe

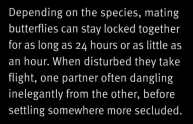

Depending on the species, mating butterflies can stay locked together for as long as 24 hours or as little as an hour. When disturbed they take flight, one partner often dangling inelegantly from the other, before settling somewhere more secluded.

△ Idas blues (*Plebejus idas*), Europe

EGG LAYING

A female butterfly can store her partner's sperm within her abdomen for many days, giving her plenty of time to find a site for her eggs. Some butterflies merely scatter their eggs from the air, a tactic that works well if the caterpillars feed on grass, but most are more discriminating and must search carefully for the right kind of plant. Having spotted a plant that looks right from the air, the female typically lands and carries out a series of checks. She may assess the condition of the plant by looking at how green and succulent the leaves are. She may tap the leaves with her antennae or scratch them with her feet to check for particular chemicals that tell her the plant is suitable. Sometimes butterflies flutter from leaf to leaf as though grading each one. If the plant passes all the tests—or if the female is in a desperate hurry—she begins to lay.

△ A violet copper (*Lycaena helle)* lays on meadow bistort (*Polygonum bistorta*). To hide the eggs from view, butterflies often bend the abdomen around to the underside of the leaf.

◁ Unable to fly and barely able to
walk, the bloated, wingless female
of the vaporer moth (*Orgyia antiqua*)
spends her whole adult life next to
the cocoon from which she emerged.
She releases a scent to attract the
tawny-colored male to mate.

△ After mating, the female vaporer lays her eggs on the remains
of her cocoon and then dies. The eggs remain dormant over winter
before hatching into very hairy caterpillars.

◁ A female emperor moth (*Saturnia pavonia*) perches on a sprig of blackthorn (*Prunus spinosa*) while she searches for a suitable place to lay her eggs. Blackthorn is one of a wide range of food plants eaten by emperor moth caterpillars.

" In April one year I found caterpillars of the beautiful emperor moth and took several home to rear them. They formed cocoons in fall, and the next spring a female hatched out. I put her in my garden, and within a few minutes three males had appeared and were flying around her. She mated and later laid her eggs on a blackthorn tree, allowing me to take some of these close-ups. "

△ The female emperor moth uses a tubular organ at the end of her abdomen called the ovipositor to glue her eggs neatly to the twig.

△ The eggs are held in place by a sticky gum that can also pull hairs off the female's abdomen.

LIFE SPANS

Butterflies are not built to lead long lives. Their liquid diet consists of little besides sugary fluids and most parts of their body are unable to make the new cells needed for growth or self-repair. Within a few weeks of emerging, many butterflies begin to show their age. Skirmishes with other butterflies and collisions with plants and spider-webs take their toll on the wings, which become ratty and frayed, the beautiful colors fading as scales wear off. Even if a butterfly avoids mishaps, predators, and the vagaries of the weather, old age or starvation will claim its life within a month or so. There are exceptions: butterflies that spend winter dormant can live for up to a year, though they are inactive most of the time. Passionvine butterflies (*Heliconius*) in tropical America lead active lives as long as 90 days. Their secret may be in their diet: the adults feed on pollen, a rich source of protein that they use both to sustain the body and to increase egg production.

◁▽ Peacocks (*Inachis io*)
can survive for nearly a year as
adults by spending fall and winter
dormant, but the ravages of time
become obvious toward the end.

▷ Passionvine butterflies such as the postman (*Heliconius erato*) lead the longest active adult lives of all butterflies thanks to their protein-rich diet. They gather pollen from flowers with their proboscis and then soak it with a digestive fluid, turning the precious proteins into a nutritious soup of amino acids.

defense strategies

Butterflies and moths use many diverse and ingenious means
of self-defense, from camouflage to chemical weapons.

△ The bold orange of this Costa Rican saturniid
moth (*Eacles ormondei*) may suggest to predators
that the moth is distasteful. ▷ Camouflage
often relies on context, as the perch of this giant
sphinx moth (*Cocytius antaeus*) illustrates.

The lives of butterflies are a battle against
enormous odds. A mother may lay as
many as 300 eggs, but on average only
two of her offspring will survive the
perilous journey through life to become
parents themselves. Many fall prey to
disease or parasites, but perhaps the
greatest danger comes from predators.
To a predator, the average caterpillar is a
plump, defenseless meal, unable to flee
or fight back. A caterpillar's best survival
strategy is usually to stay out of sight.

Adults face a different dilemma. They
must broadcast their presence to mates
yet also avoid the attention of predators.
For this reason, most moths stay hidden
until nightfall and use scent as a primary
means of attraction. Butterflies, however,
are active by day and their adversaries
are more likely to hunt by sight. Some
butterflies avoid unwanted attention with
dual-purpose wings: brilliant on top but
less conspicuous underneath. Other
butterflies make no attempt to hide.

The enchanting designs of such butterflies'
wings are not solely aimed at mates, whose
compound eyes are in any case unable to
resolve fine details. Eye-catching designs
and vibrant colors are often a message to
predators—a warning of hidden danger.

Concealment is the first line of defense for most butterflies and moths. The very smallest moths and caterpillars are able to squeeze into crevices or burrow into leaves, but large adults are encumbered by fragile wings and must hide in the open. Since their chief predators—birds—hunt by sight, most butterflies and moths rely on strategies that fool the eye. Many are camouflaged, their wings borrowing the earthy hues and mottled patterns of the surrounding environment. Predators' eyes are attuned to movement, so a camouflaged animal must stay motionless for as long as possible. It must also choose its background with care: many moths spend the daylight hours immobile on a perch that complements their disguise perfectly. After sunset they take flight under cover of darkness, though bats can still detect the moths using echolocation. Butterflies are usually active during the day and so need a general-purpose camouflage to match a range of backgrounds. Their eye-catching colors may seem to tempt fate, but the undersides of their wings are often a drab brown or gray, or bear bold, disruptive patterns that disguise the body outline. By landing and snapping their wings shut, such butterflies melt from view.

△ Unlike most butterflies, crackers are camouflaged on top and rest with wings flat rather than folded. This variable cracker (*Hamadryas feronia)* is from Venezuela.

◁ The peppered moth (*Biston betularia*) is well camouflaged against the speckled lichen that grows on bark. During the 19th and early 20th centuries, a darker form of this moth became common in industrial areas of Britain, where sooty air from factories blackened trees and killed off lichen.

△ Bleached, rotting wood provides an effective hiding place for this noctuoid moth of French Guiana.

△ The green hairstreak butterfly
(*Callophrys rubi*) is one of the only

▷ Prominent veins, blemishes, and
artfully frayed wings complete the

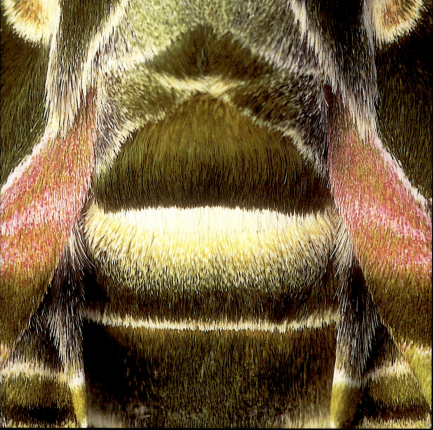

◁△ Like military camouflage, the dappled greens of the oleander hawkmoth (*Daphnis nerii*) echo patterns of light and shade in vegetation, but are a poor match for the fiery colors of fall.

▷ Camouflage is most effective when the body's outline is in some way disguised or hidden. The caterpillar of the purple emperor butterfly (*Apatura iris*) has a pale belly and a skirt of pale hairs that mask the shadow line that might otherwise reveal its presence.

△ Already well camouflaged, the young caterpillar spends the winter clinging to bark in a dormant state.

△ The purpose of these peculiar horns is unclear—possibly predators mistake them for the stalked eyes of a slug.

Girdled by silk, a brimstone caterpillar (*Gonepteryx rhamni*) prepares to pupate. Unlike adult butterflies, caterpillars and pupae are often a vibrant green for camouflage among leaves.

◁ The wings of New Guinea's peacock jewel (*Hypochrysops pythias*) are deep blue on top, but underneath bear disruptive patterns that help camouflage the butterfly's outline.

" In the rainforest of New Guinea I kept seeing a tiny butterfly with wings of the deepest, iridescent blue that glittered like jewels in the sun. The nervous little peacock jewel butterfly flitted around with maddening swiftness; my eyes could barely follow it as the sparkling color flashed on and off with each wingbeat. If I tried to get close enough for a picture, it shot up into the canopy and disappeared. Finally, one damp and chilly morning, I found the blue butterfly sitting still. Now I could appreciate the intricate beauty of the undersides of its wings: bold red and black strokes flanked by iridescent green in a disruptive pattern that fools the eye, making the butterfly vanish when its wings are closed. I took a handful of shots and then my little jewel flew away. "

△ Zebra stripes help hide the shape of this blue satyr (*Cepheuptychia cephus*) from Colombia.

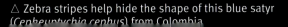

△ Charaxes (*Charaxes brutus*), Uganda

△ Pearl-bordered fritillary (*Clossiana euphrosyne*), Europe

△ Southern festoon (*Zerynthia polyxena*), Europe

△ Marbled white (*Melanargia galathea*), Europe

△ Map (*Araschnia levana*), Europe

The bold lines and abstract geometry of disruptive patterns are thought to confuse the eyes of predators, distracting attention from a butterfly's true shape. The camouflage works well in forest habitats, where it echoes patterns of dappled light and shade.

△ Grizzled skipper (*Pyrgus malvae*), Europe

DISGUISE

While many butterflies and moths bear a passing resemblance to leaves, a few have perfected this form of deception and sport prominent leaf veins, leafstalks, and blemishes that simulate spots of mold or holes. The great advantage of this highly refined form of camouflage is that the disguise works everywhere. Other camouflaged animals require a matching background, but a dead leaf or a broken twig looks unappealing to a bird wherever it lies. Imitation of leaves or twigs is common in pupae, which have no means of escape from predators and so rely heavily on camouflage. Equally unappealing to birds are the caterpillars of swallowtails and alder moths, which are almost perfect replicas of bird droppings. But perhaps the strangest form of camouflage is used by rainforest butterflies such as Danainae, whose pupae have a polished, mirrorlike finish that reflects the surrounding vegetation, helping them melt into the forest. Hanging from rain-sodden leaves, the pupae resemble gleaming droplets of water.

◁ Fake leaf veins and blemishes make the brimstone (*Gonepteryx rhamni*) a convincing leaf mimic. When it perches among leaves, its pale wings reflect the surrounding hues, keeping it hidden from sight.

△ This sulphur (*Phoebis rurina*) in Peru is disguised as a decaying leaf, complete with specks of white "mold."

◁△ These two unrelated species, a sphinx moth (*Eumorpha capronnieri*) from French Guiana and a looper moth (Geometridae) from Colombia, have evolved strikingly similar colors. The patterns might seem out of place against fresh green leaves, but predators doubtless mistake them for the dead leaves that fall continuously from the forest canopy.

◁ A comma butterfly (*Polygonia c-album*) perches on a sedge plant. With its scalloped wings closed, the comma is almost indistinguishable from a decaying oak leaf.

△ The butterfly derives its common name from the comma-shaped white mark, resembling a hole in a dead leaf, on the underside of its wings.

△ The upper sides of the comma's wings are vibrant orange and black, in stark contrast to the camouflaged undersides.

" Camouflage is often so effective that you don't see the animal until you literally bump into it. In Borneo I was trying to get a close-up of a carnivorous pitcher plant when the lens of my camera brushed against what I thought was a dead leaf. It wriggled aside and revealed itself to be a large, handsome hawkmoth, its wings slightly curled as though desiccated and with dark lines mimicking the central veins of real leaves. It looked just like any of the dead leaves that lie scattered around the rainforest. "

△ Frayed edges make the herald (*Scoliopteryx libatrix*) look like a half-eaten leaf.

△ A hawkmoth (*Hippotion boerhaviae*) rests on a pitcher plant in the Borneo highlands, its tapering wings a perfect match for typical rainforest leaves.

▷ With forewings and hind wings spread so that the patterns line up, this noctuid moth (*Gorgonia superba*) from Peru becomes just another dead leaf on the forest floor.

△ The unusual wings of plume moths (Pterophoridae) roll up tightly to mimic twigs or blades of grass.

△ The buff-tip moth (*Phalera bucephala*) bears an uncanny resemblance to a snapped birch twig.

◁ Hiding under the legs of this spectacular green birdwing butterfly (*Ornithoptera priamus*) in New Guinea is a far less conspicuous moth caterpillar, camouflaged against the bark.

No matter how well camouflaged a butterfly may be, at some point it must leave its hiding place and risk detection. Butterflies are conspicuous insects. Often large, flamboyant, and slow-flying, they are a magnet for the eyes of predators, especially birds. A bird's principal weapon is its beak; to cripple prey as quickly as possible, a bird directs pecks toward the head, aiming for the eyes. The mesmerizing eyespots of butterflies exploit this tactic. Located well away from the butterfly's head, the marks divert mortal blows away from vital organs and give the butterfly a chance to escape with only a hole in its wing. Such battle scars are common and barely compromise a butterfly's flying skills—some species can fly with as much as 70 percent of their wings missing. Many butterflies use a variation on this strategy. Instead of merely redirecting blows, they try to intimidate their assailants by revealing large or luridly colored eyespots with a flick of the wings. The sight of a pair of glaring eyes might make a predator recoil in surprise. If the ruse causes hesitation, this can provide enough time for the butterfly to escape.

▷ To complement its eyespots, the hind wings of this Costa Rican glasswing (*Cithaerias menander*) are fringed with eye-catching red.

△ The apollo (*Parnassius apollo*) has four startling eyespots on its hind wings. The intense red remains faintly visible even when hidden by the forewings.

Concentric circles of color contribute to the realism of the eyespots on this common taenaris butterfly (*Taenaris catops*) in the New Guinea rainforest.

SURVIVAL

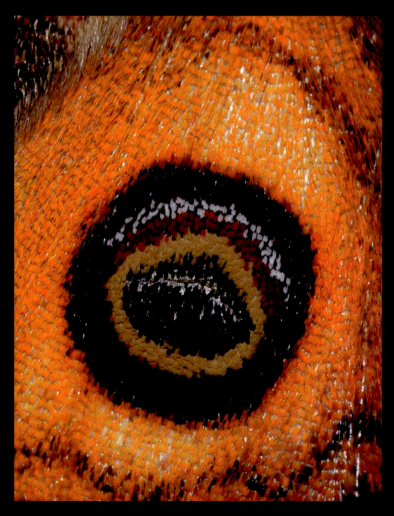

▽▷ Prominent eyespots make the emperor moth (*Saturnia pavonia*) one of Europe's most handsome species. The strong colors and the feathery antennae, which are used to detect the scent of females, identify this one as a male.

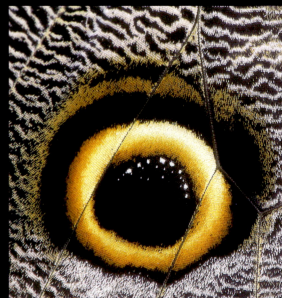

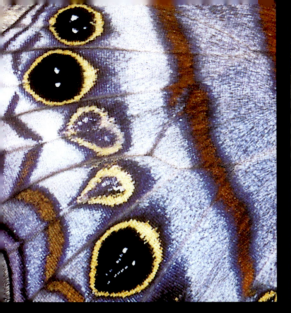

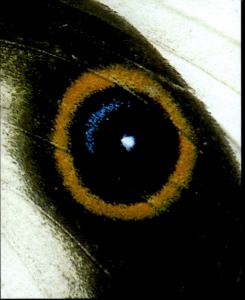

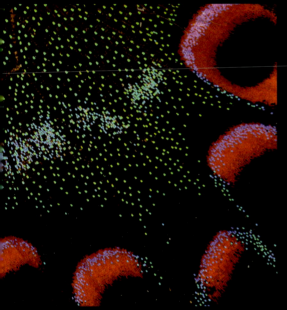

> Perhaps more than most nature photographers, I've always been interested in detail. Other photographers strive to capture rarity or moments of high drama, or they aim to frame the perfect composition of animal and habitat in an idealized vision of nature. My eyes, however, are drawn to the tiny details—the intricate patterns and shapes that appear only on close inspection yet make the microcosmos of insects so enchanting. The eyespots of butterflies reveal a profound truth about nature: its diversity is endless. All the butterflies here use essentially the same solution to one of the problems of survival, yet each has found its own unique expression. "

◁ Eyespots are far from evenly distributed across the butterfly family tree. In some branches they are completely absent; in others they are almost common enough to be a distinguishing feature. This woodland brown (*Lopinga achine*) sports a row of small eyespots along the wing margins, a feature typical of the Satyrinae.

△ An alluring blue sheen reinforces the impact of the eyespots on this Costa Rican blue satyr (*Chloreuptychia arnaca*).

△ Like many members of the Satyrinae, this European pearly heath

A common defensive strategy among insects is to look inconspicuous from a distance but more threatening close up. In the Peruvian rainforest I came across a perfect example: a saturniid moth that had flown close to my lodgings at night, attracted by the lights. With its forewings together, it was beautifully camouflaged—a perfect mimic of a dead leaf. But when my camera got too close, the wings flicked open and two large, angry red eyespots filled the viewfinder. As I leaped back in surprise, nearly falling over my camera bag, the moth flew off. It's a surprisingly good defense, and must be all the more effective when used against the small lizards and birds that prey on these moths.

◁▽ The "flash and startle" eyespot defense displayed by this Peruvian saturniid moth (*Gamelia*) is seen in a number of other moths in the subfamily Hemileucinae. Most of these are tropical species, although North America's io moth (*Automeris*) uses the same strategy.

forewings. The vivid colors may also serve to jog the memory of animals that have eaten one of these moths before but found it unpalatable.

△ Cream-spot tiger (*Arctia villica*), Europe

△ Gay tiger (*Arctia festiva*), Europe

△ Jersey tiger (*Euplagia quadripunctaria*), Europe

△ Garden tiger (*Arctia caja*), Europe

The members of some butterfly families use elaborate lures to divert attackers away from more vital areas. The elegant tails of many swallowtails and hairstreaks are not decorations; they are phony antennae, intended to draw a bird's eyes to the wrong end of the body. To enhance the illusion, the wings often bear converging lines or bright colors that lead the eye toward a false head, complete with black eyes, at the base of the tail. Many hairstreaks perform a cunning about-turn on landing, placing their tails where any furtive onlookers would expect the head to be. Some lycaenids go a step further and rub their hind wings together when at rest, making their tails twitch suggestively like real antennae.

◁ Black eyespots and fluttery tails create the illusion of a false head on the hind wings of this common posy (*Drupadia ravindra*) from Borneo.

△ Fluffy tit (*Zeltus amasa*), Indonesia

△ Swallowtail (*Eurytides marchandi*), Colombia

△ Fluffy tit (*Zeltus amasa*), Malaysia

△ Green dragontail (*Lamproptera meges*), Malaysia

◁ The wings of the gold-drop jewelmark (*Helicopis cupido*) appear to be studded with polished beads of metal like droplets of gold. The effect is created by iridescent scales set over raised patches on the wings, making the beads stand out in relief. The spots are clustered toward the rear of the wings, where a strike from a bird would inflict minimal damage.

Hairstreak butterflies (Theclinae) often sport black eyespots, fluttery tails, and a patch of bright color on their hind wings. All add to the illusion of a second head and tempt birds' beaks away from the real one.

△ Pisis groundstreak (*Calycopis pisis*), Costa Rica

△ Brown hairstreak (*Thecla betulae*), Europe

△ Black hairstreak (*Satyrium pruni*), Europe

▷ White-letter hairstreak (*Satyrium w-album*), Europe

South America is home to one of the only moths or butterflies that can kill a human. The fire caterpillar (*Lonomia*) is the larva of a type of silk moth common in rubber plantations and orchards. Unremarkable in appearance, it is a brownish green and covered with bristles much like those of any other silk moth caterpillar. If they press against a person's skin, however, the bristles inject a potent anticoagulant that can cause internal bleeding, kidney failure, and brain hemorrhage. The fire caterpillar is not

the only member of the Lepidoptera to defend itself with a chemical weapon. Many moth caterpillars (and a few butterfly caterpillars) ward off predators with venomous or irritating bristles, the effects of which vary from an irritating itch to intolerable pain. Other species make themselves more noxious to predators by feeding on poisonous plants to which the caterpillars have evolved immunity. In most cases, the poisons get no farther than a slurry of half-digested leaves in the caterpillar's belly,

but some species can also absorb and store them in their tissues or actually manufacture their own poisons. Chemical protection is best used as a deterrent—there is little benefit in a poison that is not discovered until after a caterpillar has been eaten. So species with chemical defenses usually advertise their qualities with vibrant colors and memorable patterns. These visual warnings do not always work on inexperienced predators, but those that have already learned the lesson are likely to steer clear.

◁ When threatened, the larva of the six-spot burnet moth (*Zygaena filipendulae*) exudes a fluid containing potent toxic compounds.

△ The menacing red spines of the malachite caterpillar (*Siproeta stelenes*) help protect it from attack by predators.

△ Looks can be deceiving: despite the bright yellow spines, the rusty-tipped page (*Siproeta epaphus*) is not chemically well defended.

△ Monarch caterpillars (*Danaus plexippus*) gather toxic chemicals called cardiac glycosides from milkweed plants.

△ The cydno longwing (*Heliconius cydno*), like most passionvine butterflies, is unpalatable to birds and other predators.

" I learned about stinging caterpillars the hard way. A couple of minutes after accidentally touching one, my hand began to itch. I scratched and scratched but the maddening itch didn't go away and my skin began to swell and throb. The pain lasted for hours, and it still hurt the next day. The species I touched was relatively harmless, but some tropical species can put you in the hospital or worse. Certain Central American flannel moth caterpillars (Megalopygidae) are particularly nasty. They look like soft, silky balls and almost beg to be stroked, but even brief contact with the stinging spines can cause agonizing pain. I've heard stories of people vomiting and even passing out from the pain after one of these caterpillars had fallen down a shirt or become trapped against skin. **"**

◁△ This saturniid moth caterpillar (*Automeris*) from Peru is a relative of the deadly fire caterpillar (*Lonomia*). Prickly caterpillars are described as "urticating" because their stingers work in a remarkably similar way to those of stinging nettles (*Urtica*); in some cases they even inject the same rash-producing compounds, formic acid and histamine.

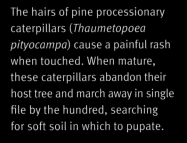
The hairs of pine processionary caterpillars (*Thaumetopoea pityocampa*) cause a painful rash when touched. When mature, these caterpillars abandon their host tree and march away in single file by the hundred, searching for soft soil in which to pupate.

" Venomous caterpillars are found the world over, but the most spectacular are to be seen in the tropics, where most of these were photographed. Bristling with menacing spines and luridly colored to advertise their potency, they present an unmistakable signal of danger. The spines work in various ways. Some disintegrate at a touch, forming barbed fragments that lodge in the skin and cause an irritating rash. Others puncture tissue like hypodermic needles and inject a painful venom. The pain must be all the more intense when the spines hit their intended target: the soft tissue in a predator's mouth. Even so, birds such as cuckoos gulp down these caterpillars without ill effect. "

CHEMICAL DETERRENTS IN ADULTS

In the late 1960s, US zoologist Lincoln Brower carried out a series of classic experiments on monarch butterflies (*Danaus plexippus*) and jays. He raised batches of monarch caterpillars on two very different plants: milkweed and cabbage. Milkweed, the monarch's natural food plant, is laced with a potent nerve toxin to which the caterpillars are immune. When the butterflies emerged, Brower fed them to captive jays that had no experience of monarchs. The jays ate the butterflies with gusto, but those fed monarchs raised on milkweed plants were violently sick and refused to touch them again. Brower's experiments proved that, in this butterfly species at least, adults are protected by plant poisons obtained by the caterpillars. The bold colors of the adult are a warning, a reminder to birds that have tried eating these nauseating insects before. Butterflies need not be deadly to ward off predators. Many gain adequate protection by storing just enough poison to make themselves taste foul. And the noxious compounds need not come from the caterpillars. Some adults probably synthesize their own chemical defenses, basing them on compounds to which they are immune as caterpillars. Other butterflies gather poisons as adults. A relative of the monarch, the delicate glasswing butterfly (*Ithomia*) of tropical America, gathers poisons called pyrrolizidine alkaloids from plants and stores them for its own protection. The toxic alkaloids are also used to manufacture a scent to attract females, and males pass the compounds on to females with their sperm so that it will help protect the next generation too.

▷ Monarchs (*Danaus plexippus*) rest at their overwintering site in Mexico. The adults are protected by cardiac glycosides—heart poisons derived from milkweed plants they feed on as caterpillars.

▽ Glasswing butterflies (*Ithomia*) gather toxic pyrrolizidine alkaloids from plants. Weeds rich in these chemicals can cause liver damage and death in livestock; in smaller doses, the alkaloids taste repellent.

Birdwings such as New Guinea's *Troides oblongomaculatus* tend to be avoided by birds, possibly because of poisons passed on from their caterpillars—though the link is unproven. The caterpillars feed exclusively on poisonous vines.

△ Nymphalid butterfly
(*Marpesia petreus*), Colombia

△ Nymphalid butterfly
(*Catonephele numilia*), Peru

△ Nymphalid butterfly
(*Biblis biblis*), Bolivia

△ Perilla crescent
(*Castilia perilla)*, Ecuador

△ Six-spot burnet moth (*Zygaena filipendulae*), Europe

△ Looper moth (*Cylclophora*), Peru

△ Nymphalid butterfly (*Eresia eunice*),
French Guiana

△ Passionvine butterfly (*Dryas iulia*),
Colombia

△ Wavy maplet (*Chersonesia rahria*),
Malaysia

△ Picture-winged moth (*Dysodia*),
Colombia

Contrasting streaks of red or yellow
against black are often a sign of
danger, a warning that the owner is
unpalatable or poisonous. Only two
of the species shown here (*Zygaena
filipendulae* and *Dryas iulia*) are
actually known to be well protected
chemically. The others may simply
be foul-tasting or harmless mimics
of more poisonous species.

△ Purple-edged copper (*Lycaena hippothoe*), Europe

MIMICRY

Rather than collecting or synthesizing poisonous compounds, some butterflies and moths simply pretend to have them. The first person to study this form of deception in butterflies was the 19th-century naturalist Henry Walter Bates. Adept at distinguishing butterfly families, Bates had sufficiently sharp eyes to discover that two similar-looking tropical butterflies—*Heliconius* and *Dismorphia*, both of which sport vivid streaks of orange and yellow on black—were in fact members of different families. Bates reasoned that the more timid *Dismorphia* mimicked *Heliconius*, which seemed immune to attack from

birds and was therefore probably foul-tasting. As it turned out, Bates was correct, and the phenomenon was termed Batesian mimicry. Mimicry is not confined to the tropics. One of the clearest examples occurs in North America, where the viceroy (*Limenitis archippus*) has forsaken the black and white design typical of its close relatives in favor of orange and black stripes almost identical to those of the monarch (*Danaus plexippus*). In this case, both species are distasteful and the similarity acts to reinforce the association between taste and appearance, a phenomenon known as Müllerian mimicry.

▽ ▷ Most passionvine butterflies (*Heliconius*) have bright warning colors, but not all of the species here are known to be chemically defended. *Heliconius melpomene* produces cyanide; the others might be Batesian or Müllerian mimics.

△ Passionvine butterfly (*Podotricha telesiphe*), Ecuador

△ Passionvine butterfly (*Eueides lampeto*), Peru

△ Passionvine butterfly (*Heliconius clysonymus*), Colombia

△ Passionvine butterfly (*Heliconius melpomene*), Peru

◁ The meneroa metalmark
(*Amarynthis meneria*) is one of at
least 2,000 butterfly species native
to the rainforests of Peru. It has
the black and red color scheme
seen on many toxic or unpalatable
butterflies, but it is not known if
the metalmark is itself toxic.

◁ When full-grown, the caterpillar of the small elephant hawkmoth (*Deilephila porcellus*) displays a striking snakelike pattern and glaring eyespots that can be made to bulge by retracting the head.

△ The puss moth caterpillar (*Cerura vinula*) performs an extraordinary display when alarmed, retracting its head to form a large, red-rimmed false face complete with menacing black eyespots. It also brandishes a pair of pink tail-whips, and as a last resort can squirt formic acid.

▷ A large skipper (*Phocides yokhara*) and a smaller clearwing moth (*Andrenimorpha*) lick salt from damp rocks by a stream in the Peruvian rainforest. Clearwings gain protection from their similarity to wasps, although they do not have stingers. Some even behave like wasps, vibrating their wings and running around irritably.

△ Clearwing moth (*Bembecia scopigera*), Europe

The narrow-bordered bee hawkmoth (*Hemaris tityus*) looks like a large bumblebee, though it lacks the bee's sting. Like a bee, the moth is active during the day.

Nymphalid butterfly
(*Epiphele orea*), Peru

Mimic skipper
(*Jemadia*), Bolivia

butterfly and moth families

There are over 165,000 recognized species in the order Lepidoptera, the vast majority of which are moths. They can in turn be grouped into well over 100 different families, based on the degree to which the different species are related to one other. There are too many families to list all of them here, but most of those that include the larger moths and the butterflies (which together make up the "macrolepidoptera") are listed below, together with their common names and information about size and distribution. Butterflies, which in total make up only about 10 percent of known Lepidoptera species, are usually grouped into five main families—six if the skippers (family Hesperiidae) are included. Although part of the macrolepidoptera, butterflies are also covered in more detail, down to subfamily level, on pages 276–277.

macrolepidoptera families

The term "macrolepidoptera" simply means "larger moths and butterflies." Interpreted literally, this is a somewhat artificial grouping. As listed here, however, the group is restricted to those families linked by particular features of the base of the wings, and does form a major natural group. While this does exclude certain large moths—ghost and swift moths (Hepialidae), burnets (Zygaenidae), and goat moths (Cossidae)—the macrolepidoptera as listed here include most of the best-known and larger moth species, as well as butterflies and skippers.

Superfamily: Mimallonoidea

Medium to large moths related to the Bombycoidea, with very short proboscises. In later instars (stages between molts) the larvae make portable, open-ended cases from leaves and feces ("frass") held together by silk, in which they eventually pupate.

Family: Mimallonidae
Common name: Sack-bearer moths
Distribution: Americas
Size: Approximately 200 species

Superfamily: Lasiocampoidea

Medium to large, cryptically patterned, robust, hairy moths, related to the Bombycoidea. Each segment of the male antennae bears two lobes ("bipectinate"), right to the tip. The larvae are hairy, often densely so.

Family: Anthelidae
Common name: Australian lappet moths
Distribution: Australia, New Guinea
Size: Approximately 70 species

Family: Lasiocampidae
Common name: Eggar, lackey, lappet moths
Distribution: Almost worldwide
Size: Approximately 1,500 species

Superfamily: Bombycoidea

A diverse group of mostly stout, large moths including many spectacular species. Grouped by a unique arrangement of the forelegs in the last instar larvae (the last larval stage before metamorphosis), and the arrangement of veins on the forewing.

Family: Eupterotidae
Common name: Monkey moths
Distribution: Almost worldwide
Size: Approximately 300 species

Family: Bombycidae
Common name: Silk moths
Distribution: Worldwide except North America, Europe
Size: Approximately 350 species

Family: Endromidae
Common name: Kentish glory moth
Distribution: Old World temperate region, including Tibet
Size: 2 species

Family: Mirinidae
Common name: Mirinids
Distribution: Eastern temperate region
Size: 2 species

Family: Saturniidae
Common name: Giant silk moths, royals, emperor moths
Distribution: Almost worldwide
Size: Approximately 1,480 species

Family: Carthaeidae
Common name: Dryandra moth
Distribution: Australia
Size: 1 species

Family: Lemoniidae
Common name: Autumn silkworm moths
Distribution: Old World temperate region, East Africa
Size: Approximately 20 species

Family: Sphingidae
Common name: Hawkmoths
Distribution: Worldwide
Size: Approximately 1,250 species

Family: Brahmaeidae
Common name: Brahmin moths
Distribution: Africa, Old World temperate region, East Asia
Size: Approximately 20 species

Superfamily: Geometroidea

These moths are mostly slender-bodied with broad wings. The Uraniidae and Sematuridae include some brilliantly colored species often mistaken for butterflies. The larvae have reduced prolegs and move with a looping motion.

Family: Sematuridae
Common name: American swallowtail moths
Distribution: Latin America, Arizona, South Africa
Size: Approximately 40 species

Family: Uraniidae
Common name: Uraniid moths, sunset moths
Distribution: Mainly tropical regions
Size: Approximately 700 species

Family: Geometridae
Common name: Geometers, inchworms, loopers
Distribution: Worldwide
Size: Approximately 21,000 species

Superfamily: Drepanoidea

Closely related to the Geometroidea, the two families included in this superfamily are united by the unique form of their larval mandibles. The Epicopeiidae are brightly colored day-flyers, while the Drepanidae are mostly medium-sized, relatively drab, nocturnal moths.

Family: Epicopeiidae
Common name: Oriental swallowtail moths
Distribution: East Asia
Size: Approximately 25 species

Family: Drepanidae
Common name: Hooktips
Distribution: Worldwide
Size: Approximately 650 species

Superfamily: Calliduloidea

Small to moderately large moths united by a number of anatomical peculiarities, notably affecting the adult forelegs and male and female genitalia. The larvae of Callidulinae feed on ferns, while their butterfly-like adults fly during the day.

Family: Callidulidae
Common name: Old World butterfly moths
Distribution: Madagascar, East Asia
Size: Approximately 60 species

Superfamily: Hedyloidea

These medium-sized moths were long placed in the superfamily Geometroidea, but appear to be the closest relatives of the butterflies. Eggs and pupae are very similar to those of the Pieridae, while adults stand on only four legs like Nymphalidae.

Family: Hedylidae
Common name: New World butterfly moths
Distribution: Latin America
Size: Approximately 40 species

Superfamily: Hesperioidea

The skippers are small to moderately large, and mostly day-flying. Their antennae are bent, curved, or reflexed at the tip. The larvae generally have a necklike narrowing behind the head. The common name refers to their rapid, erratic flight.

Family: Hesperiidae
Common name: Skippers
Distribution: Worldwide (not New Zealand)
Size: Approximately 3,500 species

Superfamily: Axioidea

Medium-sized moths, with moderately stout abdomens,and extensive "metallic" yellow or silver markings on the wings. The group is distinguished by a unique feature of the spiracles (breathing pores). Their exact relationship to other lepidoptera groups is unclear.

Family: Axiidae
Common name: Gold moths
Distribution: Mediterranean region
Size: 6 species

Superfamily: Noctuoidea

The moths belonging to this huge group are linked by a special type of thoracic hearing organ. Although uniform in basic structure, they vary remarkably in coloration and biology, and this superfamily includes the macrolepidoptera species with the smallest and largest wingspans.

Family: Oenosandridae
Common name: Oenosandrids
Distribution: Australia
Size: Approximately 40 species

Family: Doidae
Common name: Doid moths
Distribution: Americas
Size: 7 species

Family: Notodontidae
Common name: Prominents
Distribution: Almost worldwide, not New Zealand
Size: 2,800+ species

Family: Noctuidae
Common name: Noctuids, owlets, millers
Distribution: Worldwide
Size: 35,000+ species

Family: Pantheidae
Common name: Pantheid moths
Distribution: North temperate region, Latin America, East Asia
Size: Approximately 100 species

Family: Lymantriidae
Common name: Tussock moths
Distribution: Mainly Old World tropics, some in Americas
Size: 2,500+ species

Family: Nolidae
Common name: Tuft moths
Distribution: Worldwide, mainly Old World tropics
Size: Approximately 1,400 species

Family: Arctiidae
Common name: Footmen, tiger moths, wasp moths
Distribution: Worldwide
Size: Approximately 11000 species

Superfamily: Papilionoidea

The true butterflies include numerous small to large day-flying species, all with slender antennae rounded or clubbed at the tip. The forewings have two or more stalked veins arising from the main cell. The larvae are usually exposed feeders (do not conceal themselves in leaf rolls or silk webs to feed).

Family: Papilionidae
Common name: Swallowtails, etc.
Distribution: Worldwide
Size: Approximately 600 species

Family: Pieridae
Common name: Whites, sulphurs
Distribution: Worldwide (not native to New Zealand)
Size: Approximately 1,000 species

Family: Lycaenidae
Common name: Blues, coppers, hairstreaks
Distribution: Worldwide
Size: Approximately 6,000 species

Family: Riodinidae
Common name: Metalmarks
Distribution: Worldwide, mainly Latin America
Size: Approximately 1,250 species

Family: Nymphalidae
Common name: Brush-footed butterflies, nymphs
Distribution: Worldwide
Size: Approximately 6,500 species

butterfly and skipper subfamilies

The superfamily Hesperioidea (skippers) and Papilonoidea (true butterflies) are usually grouped together as the Rhopalocera ("club-horns"). Almost all fly during daylight hours (although some only at dusk), and many are brightly colored, making them one of the most attractive groups of insects. Unlike most other Lepidoptera, the males usually find the females by sight, rather than by smell.

Family: Hesperiidae (skippers)

The forelegs are fully developed and bear a large spur, the epiphysis. While much evidence suggests that the skippers are very closely related to the true butterflies, they are nonetheless a distinct group in their own right.

Subfamily: Coeliadinae
Common name: Awls
Distribution: Africa, Indo-Australia
Size: Approximately 75 species

Subfamily: Pyrrhopyginae
Common name: Mimic skippers
Distribution: Central and South America
Size: Approximately 150 species

Subfamily: Pyrginae
Common name: Flats and tree skippers
Distribution: Mainly South America
Size: Approximately 1,000 species

Subfamily: Heteropterinae
Common name: Checkered skippers
Distribution: New World, north temperate region
Size: Approximately 150 species

Subfamily: Trapezitinae
Common name: Ochers
Distribution: Australia, New Guinea
Size: Approximately 60 species

Subfamily: Hesperiinae
Common name: Swifts and skippers
Distribution: Worldwide
Size: Approximately 3,000 species

Family: Papilionidae

The only true butterflies to have a fully developed foreleg with an epiphysis (spur). Mostly large and attractive, many have the striking hindwing tails. Larvae have a unique forked organ, the osmeterium, that extends out when they feel threatened.

Subfamily: Baroniinae
Common name: Baronia
Distribution: Mexico
Size: 1 species

Subfamily: Parnassiinae
Common name: Apollos
Distribution: North temperate region, Himalayas
Size: Approximately 70 species

Subfamily: Papilioninae
Common name: Swallowtails and birdwings
Distribution: Worldwide except New Zealand
Size: Approximately 500 species

Family: Pieridae

Medium-sized butterflies, most with rounded, predominantly white, yellow, or orange wings, grouped together by features of the leg and base of the wing. The larvae are usually cylindrical, mostly green, lack protuberances, and have sparse, short hairs. Male Pieridae are often avid mud-puddlers.

Subfamily: Dismorphiinae
Common name: Wood whites
Distribution: South America, north temperate region
Size: Approximately 100 species

Subfamily: Pseudopontiinae
Common name: Frail whites
Distribution: African rainforest
Size: 1 species

Subfamily: Coliadinae
Common name: Sulphurs and yellows
Distribution: Worldwide except New Zealand
Size: Approximately 250 species

Subfamily: Pierinae
Common name: Whites and orange-tips
Distribution: Worldwide
Size: Approximately 700 species

Family: Lycaenidae

Very small to medium-sized butterflies, often metallic blue or green on the upper wings. The male forelegs lack tarsal claws, but are used for walking. The larvae of many species live in association with ants; some feed on algae and lichens.

Subfamily: Miletinae
Common name: Moth butterflies and brownies
Distribution: Mainly Africa, Indo-Australia
Size: Approximately 150 species

Subfamily: Poritiinae
Common name: Rocksitters and gems
Distribution: Africa, tropical Asia
Size: Approximately 550 species

Subfamily: Curetinae
Common name: Sunbeams
Distribution: Tropical Asia
Size: Approximately 20 species

Subfamily: Theclinae
Common name: Hairstreaks
Distribution: Worldwide
Size: Approximately 3,000 species

Subfamily: Polyommatinae
Common name: Blues
Distribution: Worldwide
Size: Approximately 2,000 species

Subfamily: Lycaeninae
Common name: Coppers
Distribution: North temperate region, Africa, New Guinea, New Zealand
Size: Approximately 100 species

Family: Riodinidae

Small butterflies, often brilliantly colored. The male forelegs are reduced, and not used for walking. Like Lycaenidae, to which the riodinids are most closely related, many species are associated with ants, although it is currently thought that these specializations evolved independently.

Subfamily: Euselasiinae
Common name: Sombermarks
Distribution: South America
Size: Approximately 100 species

Subfamily: Nemeobiinae
Common name: Punches and judies
Distribution: Old World
Size: Approximately 100 species

Subfamily: Riodininae
Common name: Metalmarks
Distribution: Mainly South America
Size: Approximately 1,000 species

Family: Nymphalidae

Mostly medium to large butterflies, with the forelegs greatly reduced in both sexes and almost always useless for walking. The antennae are very distinctive, with three parallel ridges running along the entire lower surface.

Subfamily: Libytheinae
Common name: Snouts or beaks
Distribution: Almost worldwide
Size: 12 species

Subfamily: Danainae
Common name: Milkweeds and glasswings
Distribution: Worldwide, mainly tropics
Size: Approximately 500 species

Subfamily: Calinaginae
Common name: Freaks
Distribution: Himalayas, China, Vietnam
Size: 10 species

Subfamily: Satyrinae
Common name: Browns
Distribution: Worldwide
Size: Approximately 3,000 species

Subfamily: Morphinae
Common name: Morphos and owls
Distribution: Latin American, Indo-Australia
Size: Approximately 400 species

Subfamily: Charaxinae
Common name: Rajahs and pashas
Distribution: Mainly tropical
Size: Approximately 500 species

Subfamily: Cyrestinae
Common name: Map wings
Distribution: Mainly tropical
Size: Approximately 50 species

Subfamily: Biblidinae
Common name: Crackers and eighty-eights
Distribution: Mainly tropical
Size: Approximately 550 species

Subfamily: Apaturinae
Common name: Emperors
Distribution: Worldwide, few in Africa
Size: Approximately 400 species

Subfamily: Nymphalinae
Common name: Admirals and tortoiseshells
Distribution: Worldwide
Size: Approximately 400 species

Subfamily: Limenitidinae
Common name: White admirals and sailors
Distribution: Almost worldwide
Size: Approximately 600 species

Subfamily: Heliconiinae
Common name: Fritillaries and passionvines
Distribution: Worldwide
Size: Approximately 600 species

index

DK would like to thank a number of specialists
who kindly made or confirmed particular
identifications. In addition to consultants Dick
Vane-Wright and John Tennent, these include:
John Chainey, Juan Grados Arauco, Jason Hall,
Jeremy Holloway, Martin Honey, Dan Janzen, Ian
Kitching, Gerardo Lamas, Torben Larsen, Olaf
Mielke, Andrew Nield, Jim Pateman, Bob Robbins,
Peter Russell, Michael Shaffer, and Keith Willmott.

DK would like to thank the team at MDP:
Pete Draper, Mark Deamer, Dave Bennett, and
Jenney Deamer (www.mdp-uk.com).

Thomas Marent would like to thank the following
people for their help, support, and encouragement:
my parents; Germán Corredor; the creative team at DK
London, especially Victoria Clark; Ben Morgan; Monika
Schlitzer at DK Germany.